SPLIT
DECISION

SPLIT DECISION

LIFE STORIES

ICE-T AND SPIKE

AND DOUGLAS CENTURY

GALLERY BOOKS

NEW YORK LONDON TORONTO SYDNEY NEW DELHI

Authors' Note: People have to learn how to tell stories without implicating those who may not want their stories told. Some names and situations have been changed to protect those involved.

Gallery Books
An Imprint of Simon & Schuster, Inc.
1230 Avenue of the Americas
New York, NY 10020

First Gallery Books hardcover edition June 2022

GALLERY BOOKS and colophon are registered trademarks of Simon & Schuster, Inc.

All photos courtesy of Tracy Marrow and Alton Pierce

For information about special discounts for bulk purchases, please contact Simon & Schuster Special Sales at 1-866-506-1949 or business@simonandschuster.com.

The Simon & Schuster Speakers Bureau can bring authors to your live event. For more information or to book an event, contact the Simon & Schuster Speakers Bureau at 1-866-248-3049 or visit our website at www.simonspeakers.com.

Interior design by Jaime Putorti

Manufactured in the United States of America

10 9 8 7 6 5 4 3 2 1

Library of Congress Cataloging-in-Publication Data

Names: Ice-T (Musician) author. | Spike, author. | Century, Douglas, author.
Title: Split decision : life stories / Ice-T and Spike and Douglas Century.
Description: First Gallery Books hardcover edition. | New York : Gallery Books, 2022.
Identifiers: LCCN 2022003438 (print) | LCCN 2022003439 (ebook) |
    ISBN 9781982148775 (hardcover) | ISBN 9781982148799 (ebook)
Subjects: LCSH: Ice-T (Musician) | Spike | Rap musicians—United States—Biography. |
    Gangsters—California—Los Angeles—Biography. | LCGFT: Autobiographies.
Classification: LCC ML420.I3 A3 2022 (print) | LCC ML420.I3 (ebook) |
    DDC 782.421649092 [B]—dc23
LC record available at https://lccn.loc.gov/2022003438
LC ebook record available at https://lccn.loc.gov/2022003439

ISBN 978-1-9821-4877-5
ISBN 978-1-9821-4879-9 (ebook)

Song credits can be found on page 293 and should be considered an extension of this copyright.

CONTENTS

SPLIT
DECISION

CHAPTER 1

DON'T HATE THE PLAYA

Don't hate the playa
Hate the game
Nigga, sharpen your aim
Every baller on the street's
In search of fortune and fame
Some come up
Some get done up
Accept the twist
If you out for mega cheddar
You got to go high risk

—ICE, "DON'T HATE THE PLAYA"

ICE

If you'd told me when I was twenty-three years old that someday I'd be playing a cop on TV, I'd have busted out laughing in your face.

But here I am, age sixty-three, the longest-running male actor on any show in the history of television. When I signed on to do *Law &*

Order: SVU it was just supposed to be a four-episode guest spot, but I've had the gig playing NYPD detective Odafin "Fin" Tutuola now for twenty-three years.

It's pretty fucking ironic because in real life, as my closest friends will tell you, I'm about as far from a cop as you can get.

When I was in my early twenties, I was a career criminal. A player. A hustler. A street dude who felt he had nothing to fucking lose. Honestly, the only future I saw for myself was getting killed before I was twenty-five or spending the rest of my life in the penitentiary.

Most of the cats I ran with were born and raised in South Central L.A. They grew up in neighborhoods controlled by the gangs. They were steeped in a world of violence and crime.

That wasn't my route to the street life. I showed up in South Central unexpectedly when I was orphaned at age twelve. I'm originally from New Jersey—born in Newark, raised in a middle-class suburb called Summit. My mother passed suddenly when I was in third grade from a heart attack. My father did his best to raise me on his own for a couple of years, but when I was in seventh grade I got called into the principal's office and they told me my dad had also died of a heart attack.

The thing that tripped everyone out is that I didn't cry when either of my parents died. I loved my mom and dad, of course, but even at that young age I was already in this super-isolated zone— I went into hard-core survival mode. I was already thinking, *Okay, what's next?* As an orphan, an only child, I was trying to figure it all out. They shipped me out to my father's sister in L.A. My aunt lived in a middle-class Black neighborhood called View Park. There was no love in that house. My aunt had raised her kids already and didn't want me there. She made it clear she was just taking me because she *had* to—because I had no place else to go.

At first, I got bused to a junior high in Culver City—a mostly white school—but for tenth grade, I decided I wanted to walk to Crenshaw High. Man, talk about culture shock. Crenshaw was where I first got introduced to the gangs of L.A. Crenshaw was run by the Crips, though at the time, you still had a few Brims—that's the original name for the Bloods gang.

Time magazine called it Fort Crenshaw—it was one of the most violent schools in the U.S. It was a closed campus—once the bells rang, they locked the school down and you couldn't leave. Geographically, Crenshaw was closest to the Rollin' 60s neighborhood, but we had guys from the Harlem 30s, from Hoover, from Eight Tray Gangsters.

I wasn't a gangbanger. I never joined a set. Never jumped in. I realized quickly that you don't have to join the gang; you just need to be cool with the leaders of the gang. I was friends with shot-callers from the 60s, from Harlem, from Hoover, from ETGs.

At Crenshaw, I was already known as a player. I didn't let anyone call me by my real name—Tracy. That would start fights. Niggas would say, *"Tracy?* That's a bitch's name." And shit would pop off. I always went by "Tray" or "Crazy Tray."

I moved out of my aunt's house and got my own apartment when I was seventeen. Since I was an orphan, my aunt was getting a Social Security check for $250 every month, and finally I said, "Look, give me the money. You don't want me here anyway—I'm gone." I spent a hundred bucks a month renting a little apartment in the hood, spent another hundred bucks on food, and had fifty dollars left over to hustle with.

When I was eighteen, I got my girlfriend pregnant—she was still in the tenth grade—and, looking for a way to support my daughter, trying to do the responsible thing as a teen parent, I enlisted in the U.S. Army. Did my advanced individual training at Fort Benning, then I was stationed with the 25th Infantry at Schofield Barracks in Hawaii. Spent four years out there with the Tropic Lightning outfit, firing rifles and grenade launchers, riding around in armored personnel carriers—learning to be all the fuck that I can be, you know?

After my discharge, when I got back to L.A., my friends had elevated their game: they'd gone from stealing car stereos to taking down jewelry stores and robbing banks.

Most of my homies weren't down with the violence. They were players—they prided themselves on using finesse. At the time, they were doing what was known as "trims." For a trim, the only thing you needed was a little nail file and a whole lot of game. Jewelry display cases have what's called a pop lock. If you know what you're doing, it's very easy to pick with a nail file. Crews that were trimming would walk into a jewelry store—usually two guys with a girl. The girl would say, "Can you please clean my jewelry?" A ring, a chain, didn't matter—it was just a diversionary tactic to get the employee into the back room. One of the dudes would reach over the case, use the nail file to pop the lock, take watches, chains, rings—whatever he could grab.

The whole object with trimming was to get the jewelry without creating a fucking scene—meaning, you could pop the lock, take the best pieces, close the case, and stroll out. No one in the store would even realize they'd been robbed until you were long gone.

My homies like Nat the Cat had perfected the trim game by the time I came back from the army. I brought other skills to the table. With my military training, I was a beast at logistics, planning getaways. I had a mean GTA game. Whenever anyone needed a hot car—a G-ride—that was part of my expertise. I would get cars for everybody.

I started to diagram licks with maps, teaching motherfuckers that the getaway is a hundred times more important than anything that happens during the lick itself.

The game is forever evolving, and while the finessers were still trimming, some of us decided to bring out the sledgehammers.

I rhyme about this in my song "That's How I'm Livin'."

Bash for the jewels
Baby sledgehammers were the tools
I speak on this with hesitation
Even though we've passed the statute of limitations

Yeah, armed only with baby sledgehammers, we started the jewel-bash era in L.A. Instead of picking the display case lock, we'd whip out the sledgehammer and smash the glass, filling bags with the loot and escaping without anyone in the store getting hurt. The cats who were skilled at trimming thought we were barbarians. They were like, "I'm using a nail file, nigga, and you're whipping out a fucking *hammer*?"

By 1981, I was living at my friend Nat the Cat's house on Forty-Second and St. Andrews. That place was kind of a centralized meeting spot for all sorts of criminal activity. At that time, the 40s neighborhood didn't have an established gang like the Rollin' 60s, the Harlem 30s, or Eight-Tray Gangsters. The 40s was strictly known for crews of players, hustlers, and drug dealers.

One day I was in front of Nat the Cat's and this crew from the 30s—Harlem Crips—were coming by to swap cars. This dude T-Money Bonaventure and my boy Nat the Cat were exchanging a Jaguar for a Cadillac Coupe de Ville.

While they were working out the details of the car swap, I got introduced to this young cat who was leaning up against the Jag.

"What's up?" I said. "I'm Tray."

"Spike," he said, and we gave each other a pound.

From the minute I met Spike, I liked him. He was about five years younger than me, athletic build, looked like he could fight. I dug his vibe, dug his energy. He was dressed sharp, clean sneakers, nice watch and chain—as players, we prided ourselves on our sense of style. All our clothes were tailored—"teed-up," we called it.

As we started to hang out, I quickly saw that he could talk—like me, Spike's got the gift of gab. He doesn't get high or drunk, which was always my get-down, too.

Spike's crew was respected. I knew they'd taken down some big scores—and me being older, I was always looking for some hungry young players to have as team members. I could see he wasn't with the bullshit. Spike was a slick young cat who was strictly about getting that paper.

SPIKE

The first thing that caught my attention about Ice was his voice. Before I ever saw his face, I overheard him talking some crazy-ass pimp shit—and it blew my motherfucking mind.

I'm waiting in front of Nat the Cat's place while my friend T-Money Bonaventure swaps this four-door Jaguar XJ6 for an orange Coup de Ville. I'm leaning against the hood of the Jag and I can hear some dude speaking in rhymes. He was talking with Nat the Cat's brother, Bebop Bill, and a few other dudes, and everything he said came out in poetry—an entire conversation in complete verses.

Who the fuck's talking like that?

I turn and see this light-skinned brother with hazel eyes, about six feet, dressed fly, hair permed and wavy, just spinning some kind of wild rhymes. I thought, *Man, okay, this dude's* animated. *This dude's got swag.* I could see he was somebody that was seasoned, as far as the streets were concerned.

We got introduced, and pretty quickly me and Ice—well, back then he went by the nickname Tray—became tight. Before we ever hit a lick together, we started chilling. I learned he was an orphan, came to L.A. after both his parents died, did his army service, and was surviving in the city on his own.

My background was the total opposite. I was born and raised in South Central L.A. I grew up surrounded by gangs and crime. I come from a big family. My mom and dad had seven kids—four boys and three girls.

My mother was a talented artist, a painter and children's book illustrator. She was a tiny, soft-spoken, churchgoing lady. My dad was in the military and did two tours of Vietnam, so he was gone most of the time when I was growing up. My mom did her best to raise us, but with seven kids—especially four wild-ass boys—it was too much for her to handle on her own.

I'm from the Harlem 30s' neighborhood. My roots there go *way* back. My grandmother—my mom's mom—bought a house on Thirty-Fifth Place for ten grand in 1930. All ten of her children grew up in that house, and at various points her grandchildren grew up in that house, too.

Everyone in the neighborhood knew my grandmother. They'd call her Miss Burton. Or some dudes would just say "that little Indian lady." She was partly Native American, under five feet tall, and always wore her hair in long braids. She would call to all the dudes, the hard-core gangbangers, and read them passages of Scripture.

"You boys come over here," she'd say. "Do you know that God loves you?"

Even the hardest gangbangers would sit there for fifteen minutes and listen to my grandmother reading from the Bible.

My oldest brother, Terry, was an OG, part of the first set of gangbangers in the neighborhood. His gang name was Turk. Back in the day, Turk and his homeboys used to wear pressed khakis, croaker sack shoes, and black fedoras. They were known as the Original Harlem Godfathers. Over time the name became Original Harlem Crips, or in my generation, they'd call us the Rollin' 30s.

Turk was older than me by seven years. He raised pit bulls and pigeons, did a little pimping, and sold some PCP, but he wasn't making serious money from crime. He was strictly about that gangbanging life.

It was my brother Robert, two years older than me, who elevated the game in the 30s. He started bringing the serious money into our neighborhood. Robert wasn't a gangbanger; he was the first player in the family. He taught us how to dress in Louis Vuitton and Gucci and Fila. He showed us how to get our clothes teed-up. By the time I was in high school, Robert was a giant in the burglary world. He was known as a guy who could get through any lock. When he did a burg job, he used vise grips and a screwdriver and could take the entire lock out without triggering the alarm. In the middle of the night, he'd open up electronics stores, jewelry stores, high-end fashion boutiques—one time, I remember him opening an entire fucking mall so dudes could go inside and clean out the various shops.

I was known as the athlete in the family. Growing up, my main thing was baseball. I was a star shortstop by the time I got to high school. All summer I'd be training, out jogging seven miles with ankle weights, building my legs and my endurance so I'd be stronger and faster than everyone else when the season started. I was known for my speed; my best move was stealing second base. Past midnight, I'd be in Denker Park—the main park in the 30s—when everyone in the neighborhood was asleep, with two or three friends from my high school team, hitting balls to each other.

I hadn't done anything major as far as crime goes. I knew how to "dip"—that's what we called pickpocketing. When I was about fourteen, a friend of mine on the baseball team taught me about dipping—mostly we stole from unsuspecting ladies' purses. We'd take the bus to Disneyland or Magic Mountain, places crowded with tourists, and make off with a few hundred bucks in cash or traveler's checks. In fact, I taught my brothers Robert and Dwayne how to dip and they became successful at it, too.

I enrolled in a junior college in L.A. and made the varsity team. I was getting A's and B's, planning to study real estate law, but in my first semester at college, my brother Robert put together a big jewelry score. He took T-Money Bonaventure and my little cousin Rich, who was only eleven years old. On that one burg, they cashed out for $80,000. When they split it up, each of them bought a Cadillac and had expensive chains with signature plates and diamonds.

I felt left out, jealous—I was missing out on what I felt was my rightful place hustling beside Robert. From the dipping era on, Robert and me had always been hustling together, until I got pulled away by dreams of baseball. I mean, Rich was only in the sixth grade and he bought a Cadillac Seville with a TV in the back from some attorney in Pasadena. He had to sit on a fucking phone book to reach the pedals when he drove it! Out of anger and spite, I snatched Rich's chain from around his neck. Robert and me got into a big argument about it.

"Give Rich back his chain," Robert said.

"I should have been on that fucking lick!" I told him.

"You were at school," he said. "You were doing your thing with baseball."

I was really torn. I wanted to see how far I could go with baseball—when I was at Manual Arts, some scouts had watched me play against Eric Davis, who played for Fremont High and later went on to have a long pro career as a center fielder. I don't know if I could have made it to the major leagues, but those scouts gave me their cards and said I had a lot of potential. I was committed to baseball, but I felt I was missing out on some big scores with Robert.

Right after that big jewelry burglary, the coach told a few of us that we had to cut our hair. I used to wear my hair long, permed, real pimpish. "Hell no," I said, "I ain't cutting shit." Overnight, I put my hair in these little rollers, made it into tight curls, and pulled my cap over it, hoping he wouldn't notice. Of course, during practice, running the bases, my hat kept flying off. The coach was furious. "I thought I told you to cut your hair. You defied my order!"

He gave me an ultimatum: get rid of my long hair or I was off the team. "Fuck this!" I said, and I walked off the park. From that point on, I was done with baseball, done with college. I was committed to hitting licks.

In the robbery game, I was far more aggressive than my brother. Robert was the nighttime guy; I was the daytime guy. Robert would only do his thing under the cloak of darkness, when the stores were closed, no security on-site—just using his slick skills to get through locks.

I wouldn't wait for the stores to be fucking locked up. I'd come in first thing in the morning with everybody at work, customers shopping, and either finesse them with my wordplay or take a sledgehammer and break the display glass, using the element of surprise and my speed to make a clean getaway.

In just a few months of hitting licks, I evolved into a monster.

ICE

Iceberg Slim, my favorite author, has this great line: he calls it being "street poisoned." That phrase perfectly describes players like me and Spike.

Being a criminal is a weird warp. It's an ill drug.

Once you've been street poisoned, you start turning real life on its head. You surround yourself with other street poisoned individuals who reinforce this negativity. They tell you that what's up is down and what's down is up.

When you're in the underworld, when you're living that life 24/7, what's regarded as good is actually bad. For example, anyone who works a square job is a sucker.

We don't work—we're players. We're too fucking cool to work.

Savagery is commended. The more violent dude is cooler than a guy who'll walk away from beef. The guy who's willing to risk everything and try the impossible is more admired than the guy who's weighing the pros and cons, thinking about the risks, and playing the odds.

That's one of the reasons I went by the name Crazy Tray. In the streets, being crazy is an advantage. Cats never want to cross a dude they think is a loose cannon. With a crazy motherfucker, anything is possible. He might pull out the strap and cap you right there in public for stepping on his gators. In the square world, the last thing you want is for your friends to think you're out of your fucking mind, but in the underworld—*shit!* Acting crazy is respected. Once again, you're flipping the negative into a positive.

When you're living the player lifestyle, you're not breaking the law once in a while. It's *perpetual* crime. This is your job, no downtime. You're always on the clock. You're committing five or six felonies daily. It's what you do continuously. We took that phrase *career criminal* seriously. Crime *was* our career.

The first rule of a player is this:

A player must get paid.

You're not supposed to waste time on shit you're not making money from. For every dollar you spend, you should be making two. If you'd see players like me or Spike out at a club, it's because we came up, we just hit a lick. But a player's not out spending money just for the fuck of it. You're always supposed to be moving forward.

True players and hustlers are always 'bout it. I was out one time with one of my other player friends, named Marcus. We were chilling in a club. I'm on the way to the bathroom, and out of the blue I see Marcus is in this side office wrestling with the motherfucking security. He saw a lick and he took it, slid into an unlocked office and tried to get into the safe. Here I'm thinking we're out in a club chilling, having a good time, spitting game to chicks, nobody is hustling right now.

He broke free and came running right past me. I was like, "Yo, at least *tell* me if you're about to do something—don't just go in motion, player!" But it shows you how spontaneous the game is. Your mind is always looking for ways to get paid.

Everything is a lick to a player.

SPIKE

I spent a lot of time hanging out with Ice in clubs before we ever hit a lick together. Wherever he was at, I was nearby, because Ice would *always* have some badass bitches around him. He'd be busting those little player rhymes and women would surround him when he talked, like they were mesmerized.

I was nineteen when I met Ice, and he was in his early twenties. He was like a big brother. Our personalities were so much alike. I knew Ice to be a smooth-talking cat, a streetwise player, but I didn't know how he operated in the heat of the action. He showed me almost immediately.

I had a lick up for Rolexes and I was bringing Ice and some cats from another neighborhood, the 70s. I was in a transition—at this point most of my old crew was in jail. My brother Robert and my cousin Rich both got locked up and were in jail on burglary charges. I was dealing with Nat the Cat and Ice and these dudes in the 40s but I also had family ties to the 70s—the 74 Hoover Crips neighborhood.

The Hoovers, they're like their own independent gang. Actually, today, other than the 5-Deuce Hoover Crips, the rest don't even fall under the Crip Alliance; they call themselves Hoover Criminals. They wear orange instead of blue. But back in the '70s and '80s, the Hoovers were still Crips. On the gangster level, Harlem 30s and 74 Hoover Crips have major problems, but because we were players, about making money, not gangbanging, I was able to bring them together. See, L.A. is so segregated, cats from different neighborhoods don't generally clique up like that. I took that as a point of pride: I was bringing rival neighborhoods together, putting together crews of guys who wouldn't normally fuck with each other.

The morning of this lick I scoop up a couple of these dudes from the 70s, including a tall, skinny kid named Sam. He was a few years younger than me. He'd gone on a couple of licks with me prior to this and he'd held his own, but now I designated him to do the hammer-swinging.

"When you hear the signal 'It's a good bet,' you're going to break the glass," I tell him.

"Okay, I got that," Sam says.

Any one of us could have swung the hammer, but I wanted to see what Sam was made of—what his potential was. The thing is, everybody's gung-ho *before* you hit the lick, but when you get there in real time, you've all got to respond like a well-oiled machine. When we go on a lick, I'm riding a bullet train, laser-focused, I'm not looking back to see where anyone's at—I'm counting on everybody to play their roles.

The four of us get into the store, we're all at the display case, spread out.

"Is it a bet?" I say.

"It's a good bet," Ice says.

I'm already clearing the display case, removing the small mirrors they have so customers can see themselves trying on a chain or earrings. And I'm talking to the employees. That was my thing—I got so brazen with these licks, the whole time I'm talking to the people in the store.

"Look, I need you to stand back because I'm about to break your glass."

It used to shock them. Here I am in the process of robbing their store but I'm not cursing or screaming—I'm just talking to them calmly, in a normal tone of voice, letting them know I'm about to smash this display case, so they better stand back. I don't want anyone to get cut or hurt in any way.

Ice is helping me clear the display case, he's already said, "It's a good bet," and I turn and look at Sam like, *Dude, you heard the signal, now pull out that fucking hammer and break the glass.*

Ice says again, louder: "It's a good bet!"

Sam's frozen. He's so nervous, he's standing there like the Statue of Liberty.

I'll never forget this moment: Ice reaches around, lifts up the back of Sam's shirt, pulls the hammer out of the back of his pants. Ice just takes charge of the bash, steps forward and swings that hammer like Thor. Crushed that shit: *Bam! Bam! Bam! Bam! Bam!*

And then we start grabbing all the Rolexes and shoving them into our pillowcases. We take off running, through the mall, through a side exit, get into the G-ride, and make a clean getaway.

It was my first time getting to see Ice perform, to see how decisive he was. He had such leadership qualities. Just how he took the sledgehammer from Sam, I was like, *Damn, this dude is* down. *He's with the business.*

ICE

I didn't know this cat Sam from shit. He was one of Spike's dudes. But he wasn't moving, he was standing there frozen, so yeah, I had to reach under his shirt, grab the hammer, and go to work.

That's the thing about a bash: you need to commit. If we walk into a jewelry store, once that hammer comes out of your waistband—in the eyes of the law, the crime has begun.

We started to use that knowledge to our advantage. We learned that if you pulled the hammer out a little bit sooner, you'd activate all your guys. You'd keep them from getting cold feet right in the middle of a job. Because motherfuckers *will* get cold feet. They start second-guessing shit. Once the hammer is in plain sight, everybody has to go in motion. You're letting dudes know, "We hittin' this lick—no turning back now."

SPIKE

Ice is very military-minded. Whenever we hit a lick together, he was a cat you could count on to stay cool under pressure. And a lot of times in a bash, shit goes wrong—there's so many factors you can't control. The ability to improvise is key.

There was another jewelry store in a mall I decided I wanted to take down. I'd cased it out: no security, lots of chains and rings in the display case. This time I brought another friend from the 70s named Jeff and his fifteen-year-old cousin Darryl. We needed a car for the lick, and I didn't have time to steal a G-ride.

Because Sam froze up on that lick, I didn't want to take him. But Sam knew a dude named Trevor who lived about ninety minutes outside of L.A. in a town called Hacienda Heights, and he said he was a badass getaway driver. I met Trevor in front of Sam's on Seventy-Fifth Street and he was riding a new Suzuki 600 that I thought was dope. He told me he wanted to sell me the bike. The day of the lick, I called Trevor and he comes over to the 70s in this Datsun 280ZX. Right away I can see that he's a square motherfucker who has no business being around us. I can tell he's never been involved in crime before. But he keeps selling himself: "Nobody's going to catch you guys if I drive," he says. He's so insistent, and he says he really needs the money, so I said, "Fuck it, okay, you drive."

We drive over to Nat the Cat's place to scoop up Ice. The 280ZX is a two-door hatchback so we're all piled in the back, driving to this mall about twenty minutes from South Central. We get there early, the mall's still closed, and I tell Trevor to pull right up to the doors and leave the car there. "Whatever you do, keep the engine running and the hatch open. Don't move this motherfucker for any reason. We'll be right back."

We leave Trevor in the car and the four of us enter the department store at 9 a.m. sharp. The place just opened so no one's there but employees. We creep real low between the racks of clothes to the jewelry department and wait for the sales guy to take the last plaque of rings and chains out of that safe. Then I look at Ice, Jeff, and Darryl.

"Y'all ready? Let's roll."

We walk in one straight line and the sledgehammers come out fast. Ice smashes the glass, and this youngster Darryl did, too. The problem was, when the kid swung, he hit the side of the case, and the whole motherfucker caved in. We're all busy grabbing chains and rings, and we didn't realize Jeff's young cousin kind of stepped inside the case and cut his leg on jagged glass. With all the adrenaline, the kid didn't realize it, either.

In twenty seconds, we've cleaned out the case, got all this jewelry in our pillowcases, and sprinted back to the entrance. Trevor's waiting and we jump into the hatchback. I shout, "Go!" and he immediately hits the gas and peels out of the parking lot. When he merges onto the freeway, he's driving way too fast.

"Slow the fuck down!" I tell him. It's early in the morning and the 405 isn't crowded, and there's no need to speed. He looks in the rearview and says, "Shit, I think the police are behind us!"

He steps on it, weaving in and out of traffic doing ninety miles an hour. We all duck our heads in the back, waiting for the sound of sirens. Meanwhile, I hear Ice say, "What's all this fucking blood?" and we realize how badly the youngster cut his leg stepping into that glass case.

Blood is leaking everywhere. The jagged glass sliced right through his pants, and he cut himself so deep, he almost severed his whole fucking calf muscle. He's bleeding profusely in the back of this hatchback and he's starting to panic.

"You're gonna have to put a tourniquet on that shit," Ice says to Jeff, calm as fuck. I mean, the kid was losing a lot of blood fast. Meanwhile, Trevor's still weaving in and out of traffic, going ninety. Finally, in all this mayhem, we pop our heads up and realize there's no cops chasing us.

"Man, what the fuck are you doing? Slow *down!*" I look at Jeff and Ice. "Is this stupid motherfucker trying to get us caught?"

Ice and me are the vets here, and we both realize Trevor is trying way too hard to be down. He's speeding just to show what a great getaway driver he is, so we'll give him a cut of the spoils and maybe use him on future licks.

I tell him to pull off at the next exit, and instead of going back to the 40s, we went to my uncle's house, which was in a really quiet-ass suburban area. We park the car in the back of my uncle's. Jeff stayed in the yard, making a tourniquet to stop the bleeding on his cousin's leg.

We go into one of the bedrooms and dump all our pillowcases out. All told, it was about a $200,000 lick. Even though Trevor nearly got us caught with his stupid-ass driving, I still gave him his cut. I handed him a few Gucci chains worth about $25,000.

A few hours later we went back to the 40s. Jeff had to take his cousin Darryl to the E.R. to get that leg stitched up. Trevor should've driven his ass home to Hacienda Heights, but he stayed to hang out on the corner. Big mistake.

He didn't realize he was with a bunch of wolves. Right there on

Forty-Second and St. Andrews, by Nat the Cat's house, he ended up getting jacked. This cat named Pop-Nose body-slammed Trevor against a car and snatched all the gold chains, ripped his pants, and stole his wallet.

Besides Trevor's crazy driving and Jeff's cousin severing his calf muscle, the thing I'll never forget about that lick is how much loot Ice managed to grab in just a few seconds at the display case. When we got to my uncle's house and were all dumping out our pillowcases, I said, "God*damn!*" I mean, Ice has some fast hands! His pillowcase had at least three times the amount of gold chains as the rest of us.

ICE

The thing of it is, I hated to steal. I mean, I fucking *hated* the feeling I had while I was doing it. I hated stealing so much that I did it with a vengeance.

My mentality on a bash was: Look, I don't ever want to do this again, but now that I'm here, I want to take it *all*. We're already in here swinging a sledgehammer, smashing a display case—if we're caught, we're going to prison anyway. I wasn't there to bullshit. I wasn't having fun. I didn't want to leave with a handful of jewelry, I wanted to take down this whole fucking store.

I became known for that attitude. I was the guy who kept everybody focused during the lick.

"Stay down!" was one of my famous lines.

My homie Sean E. Mac has this story where we went into a spot on a burg, alarms went off, and everybody turned one step out the door, ready to jet, and I yelled, "Stay down!" Like, motherfuckers, don't panic now—let's finish the job we came here to do. And it snapped everybody back into focus, and we emptied that place out and got away clean.

But if you weren't planning to take down the entire jewelry store, there's no point bringing a sledgehammer. Lots of times, someone wanted one special piece and we wouldn't do a bash, we'd go for a snatch-and-run. A snatch-and-run is basically an acting job with some athleticism at the end.

The object is to put the store employees to sleep, play them into putting the piece you want into your hands.

We put a lot of thought into how we looked and spoke. We used to wear Fila, Sergio Tacchini, high-end sweatsuits, and K-Swiss sneakers. We'd be well-groomed. We didn't look anything like these kids today, with their pants sagging off their asses, underwear showing, all that shit. We looked and talked like squares. For some licks we used to carry tennis rackets so we'd seem like affluent Black kids from private schools. You know, you've got to play the part of someone who can afford to buy a watch worth thirty or forty grand.

And we learned that if you had a girl with you and she was somewhat classy and sophisticated, it helped with the play. But she better know how to run!

I remember this snatch-and-run lick Spike and I did together. Spike wanted this one particular watch he'd seen at a mall jewelry store, and he showed up at Nat the Cat's place on a motorcycle.

SPIKE

I was starting to use bikes a lot for licks. I eventually got a Kawasaki Ninja, but the first bike I had was a Suzuki 600—it was fast as fuck. I came through Forty-Second and St. Andrews, saw Ice, and said, "Yo, I got a lick up—you wanna roll?"

"I'm with it," Ice says.

"Hop on."

That was Ice; no questions asked, he jumps on the back of the Suzuki. I told him I'd been casing this upscale jewelry store in a mall in Santa Monica and seen an Omega pave watch—the whole face and band were encrusted with diamonds. It was a very expensive piece. The minute I saw it in the case, I thought, *I'm coming back for it on my bike—that watch is* mine.

ICE

We loved hitting licks in malls. I'd say that Spike and I hit more licks in malls than anywhere else. It's different now with cameras everywhere, but malls were preferable to jewelry stores on the street. Especially if you were doing a snatch-and-run. In every mall, you can probably walk twenty or thirty feet and you'll be at an exit. The exit sends you back into the hallways, and if you look at a blueprint of a mall, there's like these catacombs—I mean, it's tailor-made for a getaway. All these hallways eventually dump outside somewhere. If you cause havoc in a mall and then disappear through one exit, it's hard for security to find you.

In the street, you're way more exposed to eyewitnesses, good Samaritans, even cops who might just randomly be driving by. But it's so easy to get lost in the catacombs of a mall. And there's a million ways to disappear.

We show up at this mall to get the watch Spike wants. We leave the motorcycle a few levels down, right next to an exit door.

Spike's mind works fast, and he's a pretty good actor—as players, we all learned how to flip into various characters easily.

We walk into the jewelry store, pretending to be squares.

And then Spike just put it down.

SPIKE

M a'am, if you don't mind, before I make a final decision, I'd like to get my sister's opinion. She's supposed to meet me here at two thirty."

I keep examining these two moderately priced women's watches, smiling at the saleslady, glancing at Ice, like I'm trying to make up my mind which one is best for my aunt's birthday.

On a lick like this, you've got to make sure you've handled a few watches, rings, or chains and handed them back safely: then you're no longer seen as a threat.

We always gave each other square-sounding names, too. That day, I kept calling Ice Bobby or Robby or some shit. Standing at that case, sounding innocent, as if it's the first time I've ever seen this thing, I point to that Omega pave and say, "Wow, Bobby, that is one really interesting watch—maybe my father would like that for his birthday?"

Ice nods. "It's a nice-looking watch."

"Ma'am, do you think I could see that one there, please?"

The Omega pave was a $30,000 piece—by far the finest watch they had in the case.

The lady opens the display case and, smiling, she puts that beautiful watch in the palm of my hand.

You could hear the soles of our sneakers squeaking as we pivoted. Me and Ice took off like we'd heard a fucking starter's pistol at a track meet.

ICE

As soon as the watch is in Spike's hand, we're ghosts. Both of us being athletes, any security guard would have to be in top physical condition to catch us. In a matter of seconds, we're around the corner, out an exit, into the guts of that mall, flying down two flights of stairs. Spike kick-starts the Suzuki, I'm on the back, and we're gone in a blur.

Once you're out of the line of sight—again, before there were cameras every-fucking-where—it's very hard for any eyewitnesses to give a description.

Spike whipped out of the mall parking lot, went the wrong way down a one-way, got on the freeway, then drove real calmly back to the hood.

"Man," I said, "that was smooth as a motherfucker!"

After that snatch-and-run, we decided to do a lot more licks with motorcycles as opposed to G-rides. On a bike you can go against one-way traffic, you can jump up on sidewalks, pull all kinds of crazy shit to counteract any pursuit.

There were only about five or six crews at our level, but we were all hitting licks simultaneously. Sometimes you'd show up at a lick to find another crew had gotten there before you or vice versa.

I once hit this big electronics store, and I had a crew of about eight people. It was a very foggy, rainy night, not typical L.A. weather, and it's a big night for 459s—that's the California state criminal code for burglaries. The rain and lightning trigger alarms all over the city, so the cops don't even respond and the crews are all out at the same time hitting licks.

I'd stolen a white van especially for this job. I backed it right into the store. The store had an exterior old-school bell alarm, which we easily disabled. We cut the lock on the back door and were cleaning the place out, filling the van, and these headlights suddenly appear in the fog, pulling into the parking lot—we thought it was the police. We're all on edge, frozen for a minute, until some young dudes jumped out.

Another crew of players. One of them says, "It's our lick!"

We'd already filled our van with boxes of TVs and stereos—we literally couldn't take anymore. "Look, the store's wide open," I said. "We got what we wanted. We're out." Then I literally took the dude inside on a tour—like it was my place: "Yo, here's the Kenwood stereos, here's the Alpines, here's the Sony TVs." There was too much in this place for any one crew to empty it, so his crew was like a second shift punching in.

I met this dude ten years later, after I was in the rap game.

"Ice, you don't know me?" he says.

I'm like, "Nah, I don't."

"I rolled up on you at that lick," he says. "That electronics store. I was with my clique. Me and my crew showed up and you niggas hooked us up. I came up off of that lick, baby!"

That's how the game is. Cats are out there crossing paths, looking at hitting the same licks, and we're not enemies. No hate involved. We're all players in the game. Everybody's just trying to come up.

At a certain point, L.A. got burned out. That's when we started traveling out of state. Arizona, Nevada, Utah, Texas, Oklahoma. We'd always be looking for places that were "sleep." Places that weren't up on the latest security. Maybe they didn't have Plexiglas display cases yet, maybe they didn't have in-store security. You'd go out of state and find that there were even stores that kept the merchandise in the cases all night, just covered by a sheet, which was something you'd never see in L.A. anymore.

Out of state, you'd find a lot of soft targets waiting to be hit.

✢   ✢   ✢

On any lick he put together, Spike was in charge—at least, as far as he was concerned. But because I'm a bit older than him, I might have been the only person who could say no to Spike and he'd fucking listen. He wouldn't try to override me. If we got someplace and I said, "Yo, it's not a good bet," he'd stand down.

The thing of it is, Spike had hit so many licks—and was known as being so successful—his confidence was through the roof. Sky-high. If other dudes came back from casing a spot and said, "Nah, we can't hit it—everything is behind Plexiglas," or "They got a bunch of armed security in that place," Spike was that dude who'd say, "Fuck that—I'm gonna figure out a way to hit that lick anyway."

It was like he had a point to prove to everyone. Call it determination, persistence, tunnel vision, whatever—more often than not, Spike would go out and hit the lick and then show up in the hood with the jewels other cats said were untouchable.

See, in the game, there's always this challenge—spoken or unspoken—about who has the most heart.

That's why I often say that crime is a form of macho brainwashing.

SPIKE

The game morphed fast. We were the player-hustlers and we prided ourselves on using finesse and the element of surprise. In the jewel game the progression went from the era of the *finessers* to the *takers* to the *aggressors*. Finessers were dudes with the skill to take a trim, create a diversion, pop the lock, rob your jewelry case, and you wouldn't even know—we'd walk out of your store calm as fuck. As takers, we were hitting jewel bashes and snatch-and-runs, but always using the element of surprise.

The aggressors were a whole different breed. They were the gangbangers who saw how much money we players were bringing back into the hood, and they wanted the spoils of victory. They saw our designer clothes, our foreign whips, and they wanted in. But they didn't have the training or technique to finesse. They didn't have the level of planning to walk into a store, talk calmly, pull out the hammer, bash the case, and leave without anyone getting hurt.

They started to do pistol bashes. And that fucked up the game for the players. It became like an arms race, constant escalation. And all the stores had to heighten their fucking security to deal with the new threat posed by these wild-ass motherfuckers coming in and holding the whole store down at gunpoint.

As players, in all our criminal endeavors, we never wanted to go into a place and hurt someone. When we'd hit licks together, Ice and me, we didn't use guns. If you plan a bash properly, there's no need for guns.

If you've cased the store out, you know the approach and getaway, you should be able to take them by surprise, bash the glass, and do what you came to do without needing weapons.

Eventually, on my last lick in 1992, I did break my own rule by bringing in some younger gangbangers I wouldn't normally have messed with, guys who didn't have the technique or the training to know how to hit a lick without using pistols.

ICE

The sledgehammer game only lasted for about a year. And it *was* like an arms race, escalating fast to pistol bashing. There's nothing slick or ingenious about a pistol bash. It's a full-blown armed robbery. It's a takeover. A crew comes into the jewelry store with guns, lays everybody down on the floor, pulls out the sledgehammer, and bashes the jewelry case.

When cats started pistol bashing, I wasn't with it. These were gangsters who didn't have game, who didn't know any other way to get the jewels. As players, we weren't into the strong-arm shit. We'd use our brains, our words, our finesse. It's a lot softer touch.

Here's the distinction:

A gangster *tells* you what to do.

A player *plays* you for it.

Even after the pistols came into the game, you had choices. There were still players trimming. There were snatch-and-runs. There were bashes.

The less-sophisticated cats were pistol bashing. Some of my boys started to get down with the pistol bashing. I used to call them the "long riders"—because to me they were like cowboys. They were getting a lot of money doing that, but it also started getting a lot hairier.

I mean, it's bad enough coming into a store in broad daylight, pulling out a baby sledgehammer, glass flying everywhere, people screaming, you're jumping over jewelry cases—versus now you're holding a store at gunpoint, telling them to get down on the floor.

Nah, all that extra shit, I wasn't with it.

In the game we always say, "You raise the risk, you raise the profit."

It's like an equation, and it's very personal. In your brain, you plug in your own variables—what makes sense to you and what doesn't. How much risk am I willing to take for how much profit? Do I want X amount of money so bad that I'm going to risk getting killed or catching a life sentence?

Everybody's got his own redlines, his own limitations as to what he's willing to do or not do. Like when I transitioned from burgs to bashes, one of the things I said to myself was, "No unnecessary violence."

It wasn't some moral or ethical decision; it just made sense for that personal equation I'm talking about.

To me, adding violence to the equation would only have the police looking for you that much harder. That's why on a bash, Spike and I would talk calmly, clear the display case, and tell people to step back. You don't want somebody to get hit by flying glass. You don't want to smack any employees or innocent bystanders around. You don't want to go in there and start busting people in the head with hammers. I felt we could hit a lick, smash the glass, grab the jewels, and the odds were very remote that you'd get shot.

That's what really gave me pause about the pistol bashing. I always felt that if a gun gets drawn, then somebody could be in your line of sight—armed security or even a good Samaritan—and start shooting back.

Once the game transitioned to pistol bashing, I knew that eventually somebody was going to lose their life.

Look, you go into a store and take a few hundred grand worth of jewelry, the owner's got insurance for that merchandise.

You take a life—the cops will *never* stop looking for you.

That was a lesson Spike found out the hard way on his last lick.

CHAPTER 2

COLD WIND MADNESS

I got nothin' to lose
Much to gain
In my brain I got a capitalist migraine
            —ICE, "NEW JACK HUSTLER"

ICE

Long before we ever heard about hip-hop in L.A., I was writing rhymes. It started off when I was at Crenshaw High, as a form of self-defense: I learned that using my verbal gymnastics was a good way to keep the gangbangers off my bumpers. We didn't call it "rapping" back then. It was "toasting." Players and pimps like Iceberg Slim had been toasting, putting their fly talk to rhyme, for ages. My toasts were my first attempts at being a writer, at being a storyteller. I used to call them my Crip rhymes.

When I fell in the party there was women for days
I was lookin' crazy in some hellified ways
I just walked in the corner, listened as they talked
First James Brown record I jumped up and Crip-walked

We'd be hanging out, I'd say my rhymes, and the older gang-bangers would be intrigued.

"Spit another one, Tray," they'd say. "And put my name in that shit, cuz."

See, I was always looking for ways to survive in South Central. I was a kid from New Jersey thrown into the L.A. scene, trying to figure it out on my own. I'm an orphan: no brothers, no sisters. I'm light-skinned, got light eyes—my name's fucking Tracy!

I mean, in the streets, you're either predator or prey. But if you weren't a gangbanger, willing to kill for your neighborhood, then you could actually coexist with these niggas. If you had a little charisma and swag and knew the various shot-callers, you could navigate your way through all the madness. I was known as a dancer—we had a crew called the West Coast Locksmiths. But my main thing was, I could entertain the gangsters by making up rhymes about the Crip life.

As I got a bit older, after I got back from the military, my rhymes were less about the gangs and more about the player lifestyle—I mostly used them to mack to girls. All through high school, I was reading Iceberg Slim. He was the first author I discovered who truly delved into the life of crime and made it real to me. I went every-where with his books, idolizing him. A lot of people don't know this, but in 1976 Iceberg recorded an album called *Reflections*, which had a lot of slick rhyming. I used to spit his words back verbatim. The gangbangers used to constantly say, "Yo, kick some more of that shit by Ice, T."

As far as music goes, my original plan was to be a DJ. When I came back from the army, I had my turntables and mixer and I was trying to figure out if I could make some money throwing my own dances. And then, like a lot of the most interesting shit that happens in your life, rapping just kind of jumped off for me. Nothing about it was even planned.

One day in 1983 I'm in a salon called Good Fred on Fifty-Fourth near Western getting my hair done. I used to wear my hair long and get it permed and curled—on some real flamboyant pimp shit—and while I was waiting, I'd spit rhymes to the girls:

'Cause I'm a player, I'm always clean
I rolled Mercedes-Benz when I was seventeen
From the womb to the tomb, I run my game
'Cause I'm cold as ice, and I show no shame

That afternoon, a cat named Willie Strong overheard me rhyming. He said, "Player, you want to make a record?"

I thought he was messing with me, but it was a legit offer. Willie Strong and his partner Cletus Anderson owned VIP Records, a real famous record store in L.A.

Right away they brought me into a studio. They owned a track by Jimmy Jam and Terry Lewis, part of Prince's team, the cats who'd later produce all kinds of hit records for people like Janet Jackson. It was a funky electro-techno beat. The engineer pulled the girls' voices off, made it a straight instrumental, and I recorded "Cold Wind Madness." Nothing was written; these were all the braggadocious player rhymes I had in my head. Over time, as I got more familiar with recording and performing, I had to learn about syncopation—

rhyming on beat. What I'd been doing was more like spoken-word poetry, and it's altogether different getting the syllables to lock into the beat. But that first time in the studio, my bars flowed nicely over the track, and I think we laid it down in one take.

The ladies say that I'm heaven-sent
'Cause I got more money than the U.S. mint
I ride ragtop Rolls with rocks on my hand,
Maseratis and Mercedes-Benz
I have an ocean liner, private jets,
Bel-Air bookies place my bets

They added the sounds of a winter wind blowing and mixed it into a tight little dance track. Willie Strong had his own label called Saturn Records and put it out as a 45 single under the name "Cold Wind Madness," with a B side of "The Coldest Rap." That's the first recorded Ice-T track. They put it out as an extended mix 12-inch single for DJs to spin in clubs. It wasn't something I did for the money—I think they gave me a total of $250.

Before it was even released, I remember playing the cassette for Spike in my Porsche. I didn't say, "Yo, this is the start of a new career for me." I was still a player—out doing negative shit daily.

It wasn't getting no airplay—the lyrics were too raw—and what happened next took me by complete surprise. There was this club called the Radio in MacArthur Park. I'd never even been there. But it was the only place in town to hear authentic New York hip-hop, and the DJ there started playing my record every night. The owners of the Radio, Alex Jordanoff and K.K., tracked me down through the record label and asked me to come do a live performance.

I show up at the Radio not sure what to expect, and when I start to perform the song, damn near everyone in the place—all these white kids—are rapping along word for word.

I'm a player, that's all I know
On a summer day I play in the snow

I was the only rapper from L.A. at that point, and the Radio quickly became my spot. I started to go there every weekend. I'd found my first little taste of stardom, so I would pull up to the club in my Porsche, wearing Fila and all my jewelry and acting like I had a bunch of hit records. In truth, I had *one* song out—and it was a hit in *one* club—but I acted like I was a big-time rapper. You know what they say: perception is reality. I acted like a star and that's how I was treated.

The Radio was a cutting-edge spot, a hangout for punk rockers and the new wave groups. That's where I met people like Madonna and Malcolm McLaren. They were some of the first white people who connected to hip-hop; bands like Blondie and the Clash were some of the first to be influenced by rapping and our street fashion.

At this time, the hood didn't know the Radio existed. My friends like Spike were hanging out at player spots like Carolina West, or at shows and parties produced by Uncle Jamm's Army for the very influential L.A. dance scene. I remember the first time I told my homies to come with me to the Radio.

"What the fuck is the Radio?" they said.

"It's a club by MacArthur Park," I said. They all looked at me kind of skeptical, like, *What the fuck is Tray talkin' 'bout?* until I added: "Dig, they got white girls there."

Dudes like Spike came down, teed-up, fly Italian shoes, wearing all kinds of crazy jewelry. The most expensive rides parked out front were ours. We were street dudes, players, but we had all the trappings of stardom already.

If you want to see the look and vibe of that era, *Breakin'*, one of the earliest hip-hop movies, was filmed inside the Radio. I've got a cameo as the MC. Me and this DJ called the Glove did a track called "Reckless." Again, it was another electro-funk party jam. Years later, Eminem said it was the first rap record he ever heard. I hadn't found my own voice yet, what you'd recognize as my distinctive rapping style. That's a big part of development as an MC.

One thing that's very authentic is the way I'm dressed in the movie. We were wearing Louis Vuitton and Yves Saint Laurent long before any cats in the hood had even heard of them. We taught the hood about Gucci and Fendi and Neiman Marcus. In *Breakin'*, I'm wearing a Neiman Marcus cap. That wasn't a hip-hop look. Kangol was the cap all the B-boys rocked. I'm wearing a Neiman Marcus cap because that's the shit we used to steal!

Over time I started to run the stage at the Radio—I'd introduce performers and try out my new rhymes. It was where I practiced my craft in front of a live crowd. The hip-hop culture was so new to everyone—especially out on the West Coast—you just tried to figure out where you could fit in. Whether you thought you could be a graffiti artist, break-dancer, DJ, or rapper, the doors were wide open—and you tried your luck at it. I happened to find my niche as an MC at the Radio.

Back then, you were into hip-hop for the love of the culture. It was truly about the art form, more so than now, where kids see it as a viable way to make money. I often say that when I started out, no rapper had made enough money to even buy a car.

Now, I was out getting pulled in two different directions. Still out doing all this negative shit during the week, jewel bashes and burglarizing stores, and then I show up at the Radio on the weekend and play the role of a star. That's what most criminals want anyway: to be stars. They want that ego boost. People in the hood saying, "Yo, he's the cat who hit the biggest jewel lick." It's negative attention, but it's still attention.

Most of my player friends were pressuring me to stay in the game: "Ice, why you gonna waste your time with that rap bullshit?" they said. "Player, you better come get this money."

See, it wasn't the same way the streets embrace rap now. The early rap records seemed goofy to the street cats. Hip-hop was just about dancing and partying. I was the one who injected the L.A. street shit into rap, when I made "6 'N the Mornin'." Prior to that, street dudes weren't hearing rappers talking about gangs, guns, prison. They were just hearing throw-your-hands-in-the-air party music. Street cats in South Central didn't connect to the Fat Boys, but they could connect to "6 'N the Mornin'." And a little while after me came artists like N.W.A and Too $hort.

Performing and hanging out at the Radio, I started liking this positive attention more than whatever status I had built up in my criminal exploits. Bit by bit, I felt myself being pulled away from the game.

I remember one time Spike rolled through when I was at Nat the Cat's place and he said he had a lick up. I told him, "Nah, man, I ain't with it."

I wasn't thinking of leaving the game for good, but I was already getting bitten by that little taste of fame I found at the Radio.

I could feel myself slipping away into another life.

SPIKE

Since Ice was focusing on his music and moving away from hitting licks, I found myself going out of state with Cousin Rich and some players like Diamond X, another close friend of Ice's. I didn't think Ice had made any big decision to go legit—I figured he was just taking a break from the game.

In November 1983, me and Rich and Diamond X went up to Seattle to do this jewelry bash. We were right there at the display case; I had the sledgehammer ready, but there was a guy who looked like a cop nearby. Wasn't a good bet.

We figure we'll fly back to L.A. and come hit the lick another time. But then X gets apprehended at the airport while trying to buy our tickets with a stolen credit card, and when Cousin Rich follows him in, he gets locked up, too. I barely got my ass out of there in the rental car. I drive from Seattle all the way back to L.A. Since Rich is still a juvenile, I know he's going to be okay—in fact, his mom ended up going straight up to Seattle to get him out of the jam—but Diamond X is definitely going to need some bail money.

That was part of the code: if a player in your crew gets locked up, you're supposed to be there to help out financially. That whole long-ass drive I'm looking for another lick so I can drop some money off for X's family.

I'm on the 101 Highway, cutting past Santa Barbara, and I stop off in an upscale community called Montecito. I scope the place out and see this mall with a high-end jewelry store. There's this Christmas display window near one of the mall's exits, filled with Rolexes and diamonds—I case the place out carefully. Looks like a perfect lick.

I line it up to do the bash with my cousin Rich as soon as he's free from that credit card bullshit in Seattle. It's a Monday night, mid-December 1983. We've got the Adidas sports bag, a sledgehammer, and our gardening gloves—we called them "brownies." Once we're in motion there's no fucking stopping us. We've got a G-ride. I gave this crackhead a bag of rocks to steal a deuce and a quarter—that's a Buick Electra 225—but the shit is out of alignment and breaks down before we can even get on the freeway. Again, we've got to improvise.

"Why don't we rent us a limousine?" I said.

We did business with this one limousine company in South Central. A lot of times after we hit a lick, we used to rent stretch limos, just driving around the neighborhood celebrating, drinking champagne, acting like we were ballers. No one had ever tried using a limo as the actual getaway vehicle, but I figured, why the fuck not?

We plan to park the limousine near the mall in Montecito. All we need is a second car to do the switch. Rich goes and borrows a Mustang from this chick named Michelle—a square girl in the military who Rich was messing with.

Now we hit the freeway, I'm in the back of a white stretch Lincoln Continental, and Rich is following in this chick's Mustang. We get up to Ventura County, pull the limousine onto this cul-de-sac filled with gated mansions, Benzes, Jaguars, and BMWs. Perfect surroundings—I mean, the limo doesn't look out of place. The chauffeur was a middle-aged Black dude we knew well named Percy. We didn't give him all the details, but we had to let Percy know we were up to something and would take care of him with a cut of the merchandise. Me and Rich taped a rag over the license plate of the Mustang; then we pull into the mall parking lot, leave the engine running and the doors unlocked so we can make a fast escape.

We're both wearing sweatsuits and our brownies and I pull my terry-cloth cap down so the brim covers my eyes. I've got the sledgehammer inside the Adidas bag, and we enter through the side fire doors. The jewelry display case is right there by the exit. There's a Christmas tree ornament with a whole array of Rolexes, diamond bracelets, Krugerrand coins.

It's crowded as hell in that mall, holiday shoppers everywhere, but I erase everything except the display case. Faces become blurs, voices just a hum. On a lick, I'm in my zone. I'm at work. I put the sports bag down and turn to Rich.

"Is it a bet?"

"It's a good bet."

I pull the hammer out of the bag and hit the glass like I'm crushing a fastball, caved in the whole motherfucker on the first swing. We've got four gloved hands in rapid motion, grabbing everything we can, mostly Rolexes, shoving everything into the bag and filling our pockets as well. The clock in my head is ticking and after a few seconds I realize we've got to go. Everybody's staring at us. Mouths wide open. I know they're screaming but I don't hear shit. Just a loud hum—white noise.

Rich and me both turn and bolt through that same fire exit. Outside, there's a bunch of civilians—employees and good Samaritans—chasing us from the main entrance of the jewelry store. We're moving like running backs through the parked cars trying to fake them out.

I'm a bit ahead of Rich—he's got the Adidas bag—and I get to the brown Mustang, passenger door's unlocked, jump inside, and I see Rich running right past me. *What the fuck?* Then I realize I'm in the wrong car! What are the odds? A nearly identical brown Mustang is parked two rows over, with the doors also unlocked.

Now I'm trapped—three or four guys surround the Mustang I'm in, banging on the windows—so I start talking like a square, pretend like I'm surrendering: "Okay, you got me, you got me! I give up!" But when I go to open the door, I smash it hard into the body of this big white dude, then I break out toward Rich in our actual getaway car. Before I can jump in the passenger side, these guys are grabbing on me, tackling me, yanking on my legs, and I just jump on the bumper, holding on, and tell my cousin to drive that motherfucker.

We barely escaped that parking lot by the skin of our teeth. In the scuffle on the back bumper, the rag we'd taped around the license plate came loose and the witnesses got a partial plate number.

Rich drives over curbs and medians, speeding out of the parking lot and pulling the Mustang into that affluent neighborhood. We ditch the Mustang down the block, then calmly walk over and get in the back of the limousine with the Adidas bag full of loot.

The only way out to the freeway is back in the direction of the mall. In just those four or five minutes it took us to get away and switch from the Mustang to the limo, an all-points bulletin went out and the police blocked off all traffic approaching the freeway.

Cops are all over the place with rifles and dogs. They're stopping every vehicle, looking inside. The limousine is merging into traffic onto the freeway. There's a red light and Percy gets out, pops the hood as if he's having engine trouble, then closes it—but he makes sure to give the cops a good glimpse of him in the whole chauffeur's uniform and cap. He looks just like Kato in *The Green Hornet*.

We know the cops are looking for two young Black males in a brown Mustang, and when they see this long-ass limousine and a Black chauffeur, they just wave us through, nodding to the driver, while Rich and I are sitting stone still behind the tinted windows. We drive right down the center of the yellow line, get on the freeway—there's helicopters and highway patrols still looking for that Mustang. The whole time, we're in the back of the limo, high-fiving, busting open the bottle of champagne, looking through the Adidas bag filled with at least forty Rolexes. I tapped on the partition and gave Percy a Rolex Presidential worth about $18,000 for his fast thinking.

"Here you go, man—good lookin' out."

When we get back to L.A., I tell Rich, "Yo, call your girl, tell her we're buying her a brand-new car. She's gotta report that Mustang stolen."

We meet Michelle at a liquor store on Adams and Western, give her three Rolexes, more than enough to buy a new Mustang, and she reports that her car was stolen while she was inside the liquor store.

Next thing we know, the robbery was all over the national news for the craziest fucking reason. Not long after me and Rich got away in the limo, the cops arrested three members of the Harlem Globetrotters, who were just in Santa Barbara for an exhibition game. They were out Christmas shopping, left a different jewelry store, got in a taxi, and the cops yanked them out of the cab, handcuffed them, put them spread-eagled on the sidewalk. I'm five-ten. At the time, my cousin Rich was shorter than that. One of the Harlem Globetrotters was *six*-ten! I mean, the only thing we had in common was being Black. The jeweler immediately told the cops they'd arrested the wrong guys. These Globetrotters filed a civil rights lawsuit against Santa Barbara for $2 million—and the city ended up giving them a healthy settlement for the wrongful arrest.

So now the Ventura County authorities are doubly embarrassed because not only did this very high-end jewelry store get robbed in broad daylight, but the Santa Barbara Police Department was being called racist for arresting the three Harlem Globetrotters. Obviously, they're not going to stop until they've solved this fucking case.

The cops start working on that partial plate number they got when the rag came off the Mustang, and they realize that a car from

South Central Los Angeles was reported stolen and left abandoned in Santa Barbara. LAPD detectives tracked down Michelle and started questioning her hard. The cops did their homework, and the timeline of when she reported her car stolen didn't add up.

During interrogation, they told her she'd go to jail and get kicked out of the military if she didn't spill the whole story. They offered her immunity and, being a square chick, Michelle panicked. She gave up both Rich and me. We didn't know she was cooperating, of course. We had no idea the cops were on our trail.

We came up off that lick. I went to one of my regular fences downtown and cashed in all these Rolexes. I remember a few nights celebrating, hanging out at Carolina West with Ice and watching him do his thing on the mic at the Radio. One of the things I remember clearest is how all of us were steadily pumping his record "Cold Wind Madness" in our cars—I'd be cruising around in my Cadillac, playing that tape over and over. That shit was so fly! He was describing things from our lives, rapping about getting freaky with a chick at a motel called the Snooty Fox right there in the 40s on Western.

My cousin Rich ended up getting knocked in San Bernardino on some other shit—a lick that didn't involve me—and was fixing to do some time as a juvenile. If I'd known that whole winter there was a bench warrant out for me in Ventura County, I'd have laid low, gone underground. One morning in March 1984, about four months after the robbery, I'm in my Cadillac—I think I was on my way to check on Ice and Nat the Cat—when the cops pull me over on Seventy-Sixth and Broadway. They ran the plates, drew down on me with pistols, told me to get on the ground. They cuffed me and took me to the station on Seventy-Seventh and Broadway.

I was extradited to Ventura County, convicted of the robbery, and sentenced to four years. Next thing I know I'm on a bus to Soledad, this old, rickety-ass prison up in the Salinas Valley, about to do my first bid.

When I arrive, the yard is deserted—no inmates anywhere, just a bunch of guards in military-style camouflage and body armor running toward us. I quickly find out there's been a major race riot between the Blacks and whites and the whole place is on lockdown.

I'm twenty-one years old and I'm about to get a crash course in the cold fucking realities of prison life.

CHAPTER 3

6 'N THE MORNIN'

I'm a self-made monster of the city streets
Remotely controlled by hard hip-hop beats

—ICE, "6 'N THE MORNIN'"

ICE

By late 1984, a lot of cats I respected in the game were getting knocked. Spike was under. Our homie Al Patrome—known as Al P. or Trome—was under. Sean E. Sean, Michael Carter, Vic—like dominoes falling, I watched all of these homies getting locked up.

I didn't stop hitting licks but, like I later told Spike, I found myself working with a skeleton crew.

I put together this one jewel bash at a mall—I brought guys with me I'd never worked with before. We pull out the hammers, smash the case, and get all the Rolexes and chains we can carry. But I'd laid out an obstacle course to get to the G-ride. We're sprinting, turning, and every time we hit a corner, this one dude falls on his motherfucking ass. He's a finesser—knows how to take a trim—but this is his first jewel bash. I glance down. Instead of sneakers, this dude has on Gucci loafers!

By the time the rest of us get to the G, he's nowhere to be seen. The getaway driver's revving the engine, ready to bounce, but I've got to go back out looking for the dude. He's stuck below this little hill covered in grass and ivy and shit, slipping and falling in his fucking Gucci loafers. I literally need to grab his arm and help him make it up the hill.

When we got home, we didn't want to pay him his cut. "You fell like a thousand times, nigga. Plus, you came back empty-handed—you didn't have shit when you got to the car!"

Between trying to hit licks with these third-string motherfuckers, I was still doing my thing as an MC at the Radio, and then I would go hang with my pimp and hustler friends at Carolina West on Century Boulevard. Carolina West was one of the few after-hours spots around. Didn't close until 9 a.m. All the pimps and players would go there to chill. After the Radio crowd thinned, I'd hop in my Porsche, get to Carolina West at 3 a.m. right as the scene was getting good.

One night I'm there, hanging out, macking to some chicks, and I leave when it's already bright morning. I'm in my Porsche 914, and I stop at the light at the intersection of Slauson and West Boulevard. I'm exhausted and I vaguely remember half dozing at that light—feeling like if I can just close my eyes for a second, I'll be fine to drive home.

After that, everything is a blank.

My foot slipped off the brake and my Porsche rolled into the intersection. I got T-boned, the Porsche flipped and rolled a few times. I didn't have my seat belt on but somehow wasn't thrown clear—I was knocked into the empty passenger seat. The impact demolished the driver's side, snapped the steering wheel clean off.

Bystanders thought I was dead. The wreck was so bad, it was initially reported in the news as a fatality. The car was almost folded in half; I was slumped there in the passenger seat, bleeding profusely and looking lifeless.

I was unconscious in L.A. County Hospital for over a day. I had no ID on me. When you're hustling, you never carry anything with your real name so you can always give the cops an alias. I didn't even have a fake driver's license. All I had in my pocket was a fat knot of cash.

The hospital and the cops had no clue who I was, so I was John Doe'd up in L.A. County Hospital for a long time. County is not a good place to be laid up. When I came to, I was in a room with about ten people moaning, screaming. I remember watching one dude die right there in the room with me.

The doctors and nurses weren't explaining anything to me. Orderlies just wheel your ass around on gurneys. I was barely conscious but heard an E.R. doctor telling a nurse how lucky I was to have pulled through. I had a broken pelvis, broken ribs, and a fractured femur. Everything on the left side of my body was smashed.

The only thing that saved me, the doctor said, was the fact that I was young and healthy. I was strong, didn't drink, didn't smoke or do drugs. If I was weaker or older, if I'd abused my body, I'd have died in that wreck.

At this stage of my life, I was basically a transient hustler. For most of the time since I'd gotten out of the army, I'd kept small apartments—didn't have a home or family in L.A. I was the opposite of Spike, who had a mom and dad and all kinds of brothers and sisters and cousins in town. That was one of the reasons I never got caught—if you have no family ties to the community, if you're always using aliases, it's very tough for the cops to figure out who you are.

And if I didn't see homies for a week or two, it was no big deal. In the age before cell phones, text messaging, social media, people didn't keep tabs on each other's whereabouts like they do now.

When I was in County, it took a long time for anyone to realize I was even gone. The people I spent the most time with were players and hustlers I'd see in the clubs. They act like they love you when you're all out partying, but if you don't show up for a few weeks, it's not like they give a fuck.

I was so badly injured, I needed constant cycles of pain medication. I remember lying there and one afternoon the nurse didn't give me my pills during her rounds. As if a switch had gone off, the pain suddenly kicked in, and I could feel every broken bone, every bruise, every single nerve ending. I was screaming, kicking over trays, wilding out, but the nurse still wouldn't give me the meds. All they did was wheel me out into the middle of the floor so I couldn't kick anyone.

I thought I was dying. Then, at the end of the four hours, the nurse came to find me screaming and flailing. Finally, she gave me my pills. I gulped them down and instantly felt myself melting away into this euphoric state.

I ended up lying there as a John Doe in L.A. County for several weeks, until Sean E. Mac's mother realized I was missing; somehow or other, she tracked me down. His moms told everyone at County that I'd done four years of military service, and just like that, they put me in an ambulance and transferred me to the Veterans Administration Hospital over in Westwood. I had a private room and better care and could begin to heal.

I was in traction for ten straight weeks at the V.A. Hospital. Completely immobile. You lie there ten weeks, you ain't got shit to do but reflect on your life. I started to weigh out all the things I wanted to accomplish and all the things I hadn't done.

Okay, motherfucker. Let's say you died in that intersection. That was your life. Be honest with yourself. You had twenty-seven years on this earth and what the fuck did you do with them? Hit some licks, stole some jewels, made a little paper, bought a Porsche. Basically, you ain't done shit.

At the V.A. Hospital, I'm rehabbing, trying to walk on crutches, then limping down the halls with a cane, trying to figure out my next move. There's no way I can go back to robbing jewelry stores—at some point during the getaway you always need to do something athletic or acrobatic. Some of our escapes were almost like parkour.

At the hospital, it dawned on me: Do you think you're that much smarter than all the guys who are under? You're not *smarter* than them—you've just been *luckier* not to have been caught. I knew my days as a criminal were numbered in low digits. I had no illusions: I always knew the game had an expiration date.

What were my options?

I hadn't made any money with my rapping, but I could see music as a possible way out—a new lane to stay out of jail. What really changed my mind was when I went to see a Run-DMC show in L.A. They were using lasers and shit and I said, "Yo, this is like rock 'n' roll. This is gonna be bigger than I thought."

When an artist takes it to another level, it lets every other artist know that there *is* another level.

After being released from the V.A. Hospital, I realized I had to switch up my hustle. I said, "I can't hit licks no more—I'm too banged up. Let me try to make the transition. Really take this rap game seriously—as an art, as a business, as a career move. Who knows? I might not get rich doing it, but maybe this music hustle will keep me out of the pen."

SPIKE

When that old gray bus pulls into Soledad North, the yard is completely fucking deserted. The sheer fact that I don't see other inmates anywhere—just those guards in all that body armor and camouflage running toward us with rifles and dogs—I mean, for a young nigga, it's eerie. I'm tired as fuck from that long-ass ride from the guidance center in Chino. We get off the bus, wearing orange jumpsuits, walk down a small corridor, and they give us some bullshit sack lunches—since it's lockdown, nobody's leaving their cell to eat.

Soledad is such an old prison that they don't have automated doors controlled by the tower. They've got old turnkeys. Like some shit you'd see in a black-and-white movie about Alcatraz. The guard leads me down the tier and unlocks the gate and I meet my new cellmate—a huge Black dude, on swole, his back as wide as a refrigerator.

"What's up. My name's Spike, man."

"Big Gary."

He tells me he's from Bakersfield, I tell him I'm from L.A., and he immediately brings me up to speed on the lockdown. "Yeah, homie, the Blacks and whites are at it, man. Shit got crazy. Dudes was getting stabbed all over the yard."

I'm acclimating myself to doing time here in Soledad—the wheels in my mind are spinning, because I've got to learn all this shit quick, on the fly.

Everything inside is based on your "car." That's your gang, your neighborhood, your race. That's who you live and die with. In the streets, players can float above all the gangbanging beefs and territorial boundaries. Like Ice says, players like him and me almost have "diplomatic immunity." Even if we're in enemy hoods, the gangsters will give us a pass because they know we ain't set-trippin'.

All that shit goes out the window in prison. If you're from the 30s, you're in the 30s car. If you're from the 60s, you're in the 60s car. If you're Hoover, you're in the Hoover car. It's the same with every Crip and Blood set.

Fuck the streets of L.A. where you were a player, rocking Rolexes and Louis Vuitton, drinking Dom Perignon at Carolina West. On the inside, there's no distinction between players and gangsters, and you've got to adapt to this new mentality. You're hitting an identity reset button. Behind that wall, you *are* your neighborhood. Period. And above everything else—always above everything else in prison— you *are* your race.

Because of our different gang sets and alliances, the Blacks are split up, less unified than the Hispanics or the whites. In big prisons, each gang set has its own shot-caller. That's the guy we say has the "keys to the yard."

Throughout California, it's the Hispanics who have the largest and most unified organizations in prison. The Mexicans divided years ago into dudes from Southern California and Northern California. Sureños and Norteños. Most times, they can't even be on the same yard with each other. As a race, they're organized and disciplined like nobody else. In some prisons, I've heard Hispanics at night sounding off their own roll call in Spanish like a military unit.

Those first few days we're on lockdown, nobody's leaving their cell and the only movement allowed is when the porters come sweep up the tier. During lockdown those porters are like a telegraph system: "A bus just came in; we got some new fish." They've got orders to report on everyone new who arrived and what car they belong to.

This one porter comes looking into our cell—Black dude, late twenties, carrying a broom, "What's up, Big Gary?" Then he looks closely at me. "What's up? Where you from, homie?"

"I'm from the 30s, homie."

That's all I need to say. I'm 30s. I'm Harlem. That's my car.

"You got homies here," he says. He starts naming them off, certain reputable individuals, living on different tiers.

Then immediately he goes down and tells these dudes from the 30s that I'm here. I'm still a young nigga but my name rings bells. Anyone from the 30s knows Spike.

That's the protocol: if you got homies on the yard, they're immediately supposed to send you something. All you get at orientation is a "fish kit"—a small toothbrush, tooth powder, one bar of state soap, one roll of toilet paper, and some low-budget-ass, dingy, pre-worn socks, T-shirts, and underwear all rolled up in a towel. Doesn't take this porter long to come back and say, "Talked to your homies, they gonna get at you, send something your way."

Some cats from the 30s knew me. And there were two brothers from the Hoover neighborhood—Johnny and Randy Parker—they knew me, too. Right quick, the homies sent me down a TV set, a radio, bags of food, a whole bunch of shit. Even during lockdown, they got at me. Johnny Parker was an OG, much older than me—he was fifteen years into a life sentence and had the keys to the Hoover car in Soledad North yard.

After a few more days, the lockdown ends. The administration figures things have calmed down and it's safe to let us all back into population. The gates rack, and I walk out onto the tier in these fucking karate shoes and the same bullshit-ass jumpsuit I got in the guidance center in Chino. I'm fixing to go thank the homies for sending me that package.

At this point, I've seen a bunch of crazy shit in the streets of L.A., but I'm about to get an introduction to prison violence.

Behind that wall, you're dealing with a whole different mentality— you've got dudes doing life, no chance of parole, being sent on missions to take out the enemy.

Inside, you're under a new umbrella. It's like you landed on Okinawa and don't have time to think about *why* you're doing shit— you've got to join in and fight alongside your people.

That morning when the gates rack, I don't even get halfway down the motherfucking tier before it jumps off. Five Black dudes are in front of me, standing in a circle, just kicking it. Suddenly, a short, skinny white dude approaches them.

When I say skinny, I mean he's a fucking string bean. At most he weighs a buck-thirty. Stands maybe five-five. Neck and forearms all tatted-up. By the look in his eyes—it's almost like a trance or whatever—I know something's about to go down. This skinny motherfucker runs into the circle of five dudes, on a mission. He pulls out an ice pick and starts digging this Black dude's chest out.

As this dude's getting stabbed repeatedly—at least four or five times—his homies just back up, trying not to get stabbed themselves. That's not the protocol—I know that *now*, after catching my life sentence. If someone from another race attacks one of your people, even if you're unarmed, y'all not supposed to retreat—y'all supposed to close ranks and attack that motherfucker!

But they parted like the Red Sea, so the whiteboy was free to wail away with the icepick. He must have stabbed the dude directly in the heart or the aorta because blood's spurting out of his chest everywhere.

The cold part about it is, after he dug the dude's chest out, he didn't even *run*—he just turned and walked slowly away.

"Get down!"

The police racked it and laid everybody on the ground.

Back to fucking lockdown.

Imagine, it's my first time walking out of my cell at Soledad, and I don't even make it down the tier when I see this dude getting stuck repeatedly in the chest with an icepick.

Welcome to the real world of motherfuckers having your ass the minute the gates rack.

That skinny whiteboy was a torpedo, sent by the shot-caller for the Aryans. That's like a kamikaze mission. If he didn't carry out the hit, the same sentence would've been carried out on him.

That's another thing you learn fast inside. There's a lot of high-level race politics, especially when you do time in the prisons in northern California. If a situation pops off between the races, you've got OGs, guys who are like five-star generals, issuing commands. They might not even be on your yard—they could be locked up in the Shoe in Pelican Bay—but they can still get their orders out. And when they send word on how they want the situation settled, no questions asked, those orders better be followed.

On the inside, when it comes to race politics, it's kill or be killed.

ICE

That's one thing I keep hearing from all the homies inside: "Ice, don't come to this motherfucker, man. Steer clear of the penitentiary. You got niggas here tying blue rags around their heads every morning. Niggas banging hard. You got race riots jumping off all the time. Niggas in here don't know nothin' 'bout no Dom Perignon. They don't know nothin' 'bout no filet mignon. This ain't no place for a player, Ice."

Two weeks after being released from the V.A. Hospital, still on the mend, I was back at Carolina West, chilling with some homies, trying to get back in the groove. I didn't even know there was an open mic competition that night with Kurtis Blow as the judge.

My homies said, "Ice, you should jump in this contest, player." I nodded, got up, took the mic, kicked some rhymes that were floating around in my head—real impromptu—and won first prize.

It was totally unexpected, and I felt a surge of self-confidence if a respected rapper like Kurtis Blow from New York thought I could get down. The West Coast was still virgin territory—we didn't have our own sound yet, but bit by bit I was making my name known. Besides the Radio, I used to get on the mic at Uncle Jamm's Army. My friend Roger was the promoter, the DJs were Egyptian Lover and Bobcat, and for a long time I was the only cat they'd let rap at Uncle Jamm's. Egyptian Lover would shout, "We 'bout to go live!" and then he'd play the drum machine—he'd hold two records in the air to let people know he wasn't spinning—and I'd rhyme over the live breakbeats.

I wasn't bullshitting with hip-hop anymore; I was really committed, pushing to make progress, take advantage of whatever momentum I had. I met this cat named Unknown DJ from Compton who had his own label called Techno Hop. He later put out some records by King T and Compton's Most Wanted. I wanted him to make a record with my DJ Evil E and his brother Hen Gee, but Unknown said, "Nah, Ice, I want you to make a record for me first."

We went into his studio in Compton and I recorded this single "Ya Don't Quit." Unknown put the record out on his label, it was an underground hit in L.A., and a few months later he asked me for a follow-up. So I wrote this rhyme, "Dog'n the Wax." Neither of those records are crime rhymes; they're more in the style of New York rappers of the time like Kool Moe Dee or LL Cool J.

"Dog'n the Wax" needed a B side, and as I was thinking about what to write, my boy Randy Mac says, "Talk that real shit you be talkin', Ice. Fuck that party hip-hop—that ain't you, man. Talk that real rough street shit."

I said, "Nah, player, nobody wants to hear all that negative shit."

But a couple things happened simultaneously that led me to write "6 'N the Mornin'."

For one, I'd been rereading Iceberg Slim's novels while recovering from the car accident. And it dawned on me: Pimpin' and hoein' is as old as human civilization. And there've been thousands of pimps, but people remember the name Iceberg Slim. Why? Because he wrote his stories down. More than just a pimp, he was a *writer*. He had the insight to document the game.

I figured, I'll document the stories about the real players and gangsters in these streets of L.A. as I've lived it and seen it.

The second thing that happened was that I heard Schoolly D's record "PSK: What Does It Mean?" in a club. I turned to my friends and said, "Yo, this shit is so dusted!" It sounded different than any previous rap record. Stripped down, just percussion, heavy echo effects, vocal delivery hard as fuck. Schoolly D was writing about Park Side Killers, a Philly gang, but he didn't get explicit. "One by one I'm knocking you out" was the most violent thing he said.

I took Schoolly D's rhyme cadence and molded it onto Iceberg Slim's style of realistic crime storytelling and finally discovered my own voice. I wrote "6 'N the Mornin'" quickly in my apartment with an 808 drum machine. I call the lyrics "faction." It's a fictional adventure based on factual experiences.

As I was scribbling the lyrics on loose-leaf paper, I was thinking about the homies—in the streets and behind bars. What kind of stories would they connect to?

Six in the mornin' police at my door
Fresh Adidas squeak across the bathroom floor
Out the back window I make my escape
Didn't even get a chance to grab my old-school tape

Mad with no music but happy 'cause free
And the streets to a player is the place to be

Got a knot in my pocket weighin' at least a grand
Gold on my neck, my pistol's close at hand

I'm a self-made monster of the city streets
Remotely controlled by hard hip-hop beats
But just livin' in the city is a serious task
Didn't know what the cops wanted
Didn't have the time to ask
Word

I was feeling loose and experimental with the writing and recording. The beat was minimalist. Nobody had ever used a scratch break on a record. Nobody had ever used such explicit lyrics—I kept it honest to the way we talked. Techno Hop was a totally indie label, so it wasn't like I was worried about being censored.

The story's about a player running from the LAPD, hanging out in the hood—he ends up getting caught with guns and going to the pen for seven years.

Back on the streets after five and a deuce
Seven years later, but still had the juice
My homeboy Hen Gee put me up the track
Told me E's rolling Villain
BJ's got the sack
Bruce is a giant
Nat C's clocking dough

Bebop's a pimp
My old freak's a ho
The battering ram's rolling
Rocks are the thing
Life has no meaning and money is king

I tossed in the names of the real homies, the players, the drug dealers. If you don't know who I'm talking about, it's just random fucking names and words. But if you were from South Central, the story had a level of detail that made a lot of people sit up and take notice.

I shouted out BJ, one of our homies from the 40s who was selling coke. And Bruce Richardson, a younger friend of both Spike and mine, who'd become a *giant*, a heavyweight in the drug game, getting kilos from a wholesale connect.

I'm also giving you a little criminology snapshot of L.A. in 1986.

Rocks are the thing.

That's me saying the transition has happened. We've gone from the era of jewel bashes to the era of crack. Selling rocks is the newest and most lucrative hustle.

Life has no meaning and money is king.

But with all that new drug money in the hood, the streets had become a killing zone.

Looking back on it now, "6 'N the Mornin'" was all about transitions—transitions in the game and in my music.

I was switching up my lyrical style, but I wasn't expecting the impact that one B side was going to have, that it would pretty much transform the hip-hop sound of the West Coast and give birth to an entire genre called gangsta rap.

SPIKE

'll never forget when I got the tape of "6 'N the Mornin'" in Soledad. That song blew my motherfucking mind, man! I listened to it so many times in my cell I damn near wore the fucking cassette out.

When you're in prison, any connections to home, a phone call or a letter, is like a lifeline. "6 'N the Mornin'" was personal to me—to hear Ice rapping about all these real-life cats in our circle: Sean E. Sean, Nat the Cat, Bebop Bill, Evil E, Hen Gee, BJ, and Bruce. And he was doing it a way that you could visualize everything—the way he laid down the verses, you could close your eyes in your cell and imagine "6 'N the Mornin'" as a gangster movie.

Ice was making this transformation with his music; meanwhile, I was going through my own changes in Soledad.

My mind was still fluctuating between my new prison reality and everything I'd left behind on the streets. I had a baby daughter with my girlfriend in Bakersfield. I was still a young guy, planning to go back to L.A. and get my hustle on, but most of these cats I was hanging with in Soledad were lifers. They were fixing to die behind that wall.

As soon as the lockdown ended, Johnny Parker had me transferred to his cell. His brother Randy had just paroled out and there was an open bed. As the Hoover shot-caller, Johnny was living like a Mafia boss: he could get all kinds of luxuries, contraband—pretty much anything he wanted smuggled in from the outside. And he had cats in the kitchen getting him extra beef and chicken, so we were eating good.

But after a few weeks with Johnny, I got transferred from Soledad North to Soledad South. There, they put me to work in the kitchen, and that's where I really learned about the weight pile.

There's so much stress in prison, for most dudes that weight pile on the yard becomes their whole existence. Working out becomes the most important thing in the day. It's just about the only thing in their lives they can still control. Like everything else inside, it's segregated by race—the Blacks only work out with Blacks, whites with whites, Hispanics with Hispanics.

I'm out on the yard for my rec time one morning and I see this little dude who was like the king of the weight pile.

He was shorter than every other dude on the yard—maybe five-two or five-three—but he was a monster. He was *killing* it on that pile. He was putting up more weight than guys twice his size.

Come to find out this dude's name is Jamo. Dark, mid-thirties, looks like a pit bull. He's with the Black Guerilla Family, one of the old prison gangs from the 1960s. He's been down forever; he's doing a life sentence and knows he's never coming home.

My first day on the yard, I'm standing there, not believing what I'm seeing. Jamo's got over five hundred pounds on the bench. He lowers the bar to his chest. Pauses the shit—I mean, to a complete stop, no bouncing—then he's talking calmly, with crazy confidence, just like I used to do inside a jewelry store during a bash.

"Now back up for your own fucking safety," he says, and then he reps that five hundred pounds six times like it's nothing.

The second or third time I watched Jamo working out, a dude named Kiko Cox introduced us. With Jamo, you needed a personal introduction, because he wouldn't fuck with just anybody. He was still under the constitution of the BGF—had been through decades of prison wars—so he didn't trust most dudes.

"You wanna get down?" Jamo asks me.

"Man, I can't get up under that shit!"

I had baseball strength, I could crush a fastball, but I'd never really worked out with weights.

Weights on the yard are different than weights in a gym. We call it "pig iron." It's bare metal, old and rusted, and something about it—when you're under it, you feel all your weak spots and sticking points. Lifting pig iron gives you a different kind of strength.

Jamo said to strip the bar down to two quarters for me. That's iron-pile slang, and I had to learn it quick. Those plates are called quarters—they each weigh about twenty-five pounds, but they could be twenty-seven or thirty. You never know; it's raw pig iron, after all. And in the jargon of the iron pile, you only talk about how many quarters you've got on *one* side of the bar. "Two quarters" really means I had four plates on the bar. Roughly one-seventy total. And a guy like Jamo who could easily bench "ten quarters" was putting up twenty plates—way over five hundred fucking pounds for reps.

Looking back on it now, it's crazy, because when I was doing my life sentence at the Level IV at Calipatria, I became a monster in the weight pile. I was squatting over six hundred pounds and competing in powerlifting contests and all that shit. But in Soledad, at age nineteen, I could barely even bench that one hundred seventy pounds.

I stood up from the bench, all out of breath. "Damn, that shit was kind of hard."

That same amount I was struggling with, Jamo adds six or seven more plates on *each* side. And handles it like it's nothing! Pound for pound, this is the strongest dude I've ever seen in my life.

How the fuck is that possible? How's he doing it?

It was like when you're a kid and you see a magic trick and get obsessed with understanding how the magician did it. It became a challenge to me—an intellectual challenge—trying to figure out how Jamo was able to lift so much weight.

He took me under his wing. He started to train with me. He corrected my form. He taught me about sticking points. He got me doing diamond push-ups, working with dumbbells to isolate specific areas, improving the coordination between my shoulders and triceps.

Man, he was a no-nonsense motherfucker. Jamo's routines were so intense, the whole time you were lifting, you were building up your stamina, because he kept the pace relentless. In the first ten minutes, you were bathed in sweat, gasping, trying to keep up. But if you could hang with Jamo in the iron pile, your conditioning improved immediately.

For whatever reason, he took an interest in teaching me, and I started seeing the changes within weeks. Because I was so young, my body adapted fast, man. Before long, I was getting strong as fuck. I never reached Jamo's level, I couldn't fuck with five hundred, but I was repping four hundred on the bench within the year.

Working in the kitchen, I was getting plenty of protein. And working out daily with Jamo, by the time I paroled out, I'd packed on about thirty or forty pounds of muscle. I was on swole. Hair in jail braids. I'd changed so much that cats back home didn't even recognize me.

News from the streets travels fast up into those penitentiaries. Besides Ice's success in the rap game, the name I kept hearing about was Bruce Richardson. I heard Ice rapping, "Bruce is a giant," but didn't really understand until I saw it with my own eyes.

One of the last licks I hit before getting locked up was the one when Ice said, "I ain't with it." I ended up bringing my friend Jeff from Seventy-Seventh Street. Jeff told his young cousin Bruce Richardson. Bruce wasn't a jewel thief, but he wanted to go on a lick because he saw how much money Jeff was making with me.

Bruce was about seventeen, still going to Crenshaw High, playing basketball. He was a small-time weed dealer, hadn't even got into the cocaine game yet. I told him he could come with us on the lick if he got a G, but when he showed up at Jeff's the next morning, he was in his own whip.

"Ain't that your car? I told you, homie, you can't hit no lick in your personal car."

The rest of us all had G-rides. But I didn't have time to explain shit, we were on a mission, on the clock. We left Jeff's house, got to the jewelry store, pulled out the hammers, busted the glass, came running out with the loot. I look back in the parking lot, I see Bruce standing there next to his car.

He wanted to be down so bad that he followed us on the lick. We ditch our G-rides, and an hour later we've got the *entire* jewelry store inside Jeff's bedroom, piled up on one of the bunk beds. Bruce came inside and was watching us all taking a few personal pieces. I kind of scolded him again: "Youngster, you followed us in your personal car. You could've got fucking arrested." But since he was Jeff's cousin, I told him, "On the strength, youngster, go and get yourself a few pieces." He took a Rolex or two. "Next time we go on a lick, if you don't participate, you don't get shit."

Bruce never forgot that.

Flash forward three years. I parole out of Soledad on July 4, 1986, and get back to my mom's house. I've literally only been home for a few hours, haven't even checked in with my parole officer, and someone shows up at the crib. I come out, see this tall light-skinned brother in a very expensive suit and trench coat getting out of a new black Cadillac.

Bruce?

Damn, I wasn't the only one who'd completely transformed in less than three years.

We're hugging and shit, but I'm kind of dumbfounded, because I never once called or wrote Bruce when I was in prison. He sees that I don't have any decent clothes, my hair's in these fucking braids from Soledad, and he takes me straight to the Beverly Center—spends about $5,000 buying me some fly new clothes and shoes at different stores, then gives me $10,000 to put in my pocket.

Before we part ways, he takes me to a well-known neighborhood called Six Deuce Brims. That's where Bruce grew up, on Sixty-Fifth and Budlong. In the time I've been gone, he's bought five houses on the block for his mom and the rest of his family. Besides the Cadillac, he had a Bentley, a '57 Chevy Ragtop, a Corvette. The street looked like a car show. I'm like, *Damn, this youngster is on his feet.*

Little did I realize that Bruce was *really* on his feet.

He says, "Go out to the woodshed and get that paper bag and put it in the freezer."

I grab the bag—it's filled with eight kilos of cocaine—and bring it into the kitchen. "Yo, I can't fit anything else in here, man." The whole freezer was already packed with dozens of kilos of cocaine!

Bruce must have done a deal overnight because he's got about a million in cash bundled up on the counter. He's got two triple-beam scales, and I see residue of cocaine on the kitchen table.

He hands me one of the kilos. "Here, man, this is for you to get back on your feet. When you get rid of that, just get back at me."

My mind is blown. I'm a jewel thief. I'm a taker. I know how to plan and execute a jewel lick like a motherfucker.

I've never sold kilos of cocaine.

Still, I understand that Bruce is putting me onto the new game. Everybody's cooking crack, setting up rockhouses out of state, and making crazy money.

In Soledad I heard Ice rhyming about this kid Bruce becoming a giant, saying rocks are the thing, but now I'm actually *entering* Bruce's world. Fresh out, first day home, I feel like I'm literally living out the lyrics of "6 'N the Mornin'."

ICE

As players we're supposed to look out for each other. But one of the coldest things about the game is that it's actually very *rare* that a player will help another player get back on his feet when he's down—especially when a dude's just come home from prison.

That's what made Bruce Richardson a special cat. He was very generous and very loyal. Everybody in our circle loved Bruce.

Bruce was a young player who went to Crenshaw after me. Really smart dude, one of the first players to open up legit businesses in the hood—first he had Genius Car Wash on Crenshaw, then a bunch of other businesses. He had so much money coming in, he was constantly looking for ways to clean it. When I wrote "6 'N the Mornin'," he was the only guy from our area who'd risen to that top level in the cocaine game.

Most of us had our little drug-selling phase in the mid-'80s. Nobody got as large as Bruce, but almost all of us gave it a shot. I only tried once. Never re-upped. I bought some cocaine, about half a kilo. I split it up to some friends, asked them to sell it. But everybody came back short. Everybody had an excuse as to why they didn't have the money they were supposed to have for me.

I broke even on the deal—I made my investment back but no profit. I said, "This hustle ain't for me."

See, if you give out cocaine to your crew, you've got to pressure them to pay you back what they're supposed to. But how do you pressure your *friends*? How do you put fear into homies that you care about?

Some cats can do it, no problem. I couldn't. Plus, in that cocaine hustle, there were too many moving parts—hitting jewel licks was a lot more straightforward. But by the time I did my little coke hustle, I was already trying to get out of the game, taking my music more seriously. In fact, I saw myself pushing a new product—*dope* music was the drug I was slinging. A few years later, in "I'm Your Pusher," I laid it out, metaphorically:

> *For this drug deal, I'm the big wheel*
> *The dope I'm sellin', you don't smoke, you feel*
> *Out on the dance floor, on my world tour*
> *I'm sellin' dope in each and every record store*

Getting out of the game while simultaneously *documenting* the game was my lane. That was my avenue to success. "6 'N the Mornin'" kicked off a whole new chapter for me. No airplay, no promotion, just a B side, and that record blew up strictly on word of mouth. I didn't even know the song was a hit until I got a call from the Fillmore West up in San Francisco. They said, "Would you come up to do a concert?"

"I only got one fucking song."

"Nah, they feelin' you up here in the Bay, Ice. They know all your music."

"Word? Okay, cool."

A few days later, they call me back to ask about booking another concert.

"I'm already doing one."

"That sold out."

I'm like, *Are you kidding me? Behind "6 'N the Mornin'" I sold out a show?*

That's when I knew I was onto something, that I'd found my voice, that a lot of people related to the harder edge. It was so simple. I had to stop trying to sound like someone I wasn't. Just write about what I know. I said, "If they like these fucking gangster stories, shit, I got thousands of them."

I was still the in-house MC at the Radio, and all these New York hip-hop artists were coming to the club to perform. The turning point for me was meeting Afrika Islam, the DJ for the Rock Steady Crew, and Grandmaster Caz of the Cold Crush Brothers, hands down one of the greatest lyricists in hip-hop history.

Afrika Islam was a boss. I mean, dude had clout. He was the president of the Universal Zulu Nation. To those of us in L.A. who knew about hip-hop, these cats were legends.

When they met me, both Caz and Islam were tripping on how hard I was pushing to get into the music business.

"Why the fuck you wanna rap, man?" Caz said. "You already ballin'!" Hanging out with me and my crew, they saw we had on the fly designer clothes, Rolexes, rope chains, drove Porsches and Benzes. The players, pimps, and hustlers of L.A. were pulling in way more money than any rapper in those early days of hip-hop.

Afrika Islam was feeling the street edginess of "6 'N the Mornin'" and wanted to help me get it played in New York. But because I was from the West Coast, he said dudes back East weren't going to respect the record until they saw me in person. "You gotta get out to New York, Ice."

I bought myself a cheap flight to New York. Soon as I touched down, Islam told me we were getting some good early reactions to "6 'N the Mornin'." It was a different-sounding record to New York cats. Islam introduced me to Red Alert, Chuck Chillout, and Scott La Rock—three of the most influential hip-hop DJs in New York. All of them started to spin "6 'N the Mornin'" in the clubs and parties. To hear my record getting played at jams in the Bronx—the birthplace of hip-hop—was a trip. Overnight, I had some credibility with the New York hip-hop cats.

While he was out there pushing that 12-inch, Islam was also trying to set up a compilation project with me, Melle Mel, Grandmaster Caz, Donald D, and Bronx Style Bob—one of Islam's unsigned MCs. We recorded a couple of singles in New York for this small label called Posse Records—the group was credited as "Afrika & the Zulu Kings." Islam had a friend named Ralph Cooper II—his father was a well-known actor who'd started Amateur Night at the Apollo Theater in the 1930s—and Ralph wanted to bring the compilation project to Seymour Stein at Sire Records.

But when it got down to the nitty-gritty, most of these dudes already had contractual obligations. Mel was on Sugar Hill Records, Caz was on Tuff City, Donald D was signed to Vintertainment, and Bronx Style Bob hadn't made any solo records. I was the only rapper out of the five of us who had some recording experience and didn't have a ball and chain of legal paperwork trailing behind me to complicate the deal.

Seymour Stein says, "Okay, fine, I'll take Ice-T."

That's the funny part: I basically got my deal by *default*. I was the last MC standing. Rap music was such a new phenomenon to Seymour Stein, he didn't consider that taking me on as a solo artist might be a risky bet—I mean, no West Coast MC had ever been signed to a major label before. There were no star rappers from the West—period.

Next thing I know, Ralph Cooper II sets up a meeting for us at the offices of Sire Records. Up to this point, I've just been recording for small indie labels, mostly selling records out of mom-and-pop stores. Now we're trying to finalize an album deal with the Warner Bros. empire.

Seymour Stein is a visionary cat who signed the Ramones, the Talking Heads, the Pretenders, and Madonna. I took the elevator up to the Sire offices with Islam, and when we walked into his office, Seymour was blasting calypso music and dancing around in his socks. He told me he'd listened closely to my lyrics and thought I sounded like Bob Dylan. That's Seymour in a nutshell—he's real eclectic in his tastes and sees connections that other people don't see. I said, "Cool." I mean, of course I dig Dylan. I always thought "Subterranean Homesick Blues" was a great fucking rap record.

Seymour offered us a deal on the spot. "I want you to make this album for me," he says. "I'm going to give you a forty-thousand-dollar advance." That was the great part about working with Seymour as a boss: he didn't want to micromanage the whole recording process or have an A&R guy look over your shoulder telling you how to improve the tracks. He just wanted to front you the money: "Go make the record *you* want to make." If you were passionate about your music, then he'd figure out how to promote and sell it. At the end of that first meeting, he personally wrote out a check for the entire budget of my first album.

We walked out of his office, ready to get to work. Forty grand was a tiny budget, even back in '86. But Afrika Islam and me went straight out and bought two new drum machines. We made the whole of *Rhyme Pays* in about six weeks at Secret Sound studios in Manhattan. Mixed the entire album in one night—with *no* automation.

Back then, album covers used to be nearly as important as the music itself. We hired Glen E. Friedman to shoot ours. Glen was the photographer who did albums for the Beastie Boys and LL Cool J—later on, he did covers for Public Enemy and Slick Rick. A ton of classic hip-hop covers. Glen wanted to have a Southern California vibe, so we did a cover with palm trees, my girl in a bikini, my red Porsche with the top down. At first glance, you immediately get that I'm representing L.A., not trying to be a clone of the established New York rappers.

In my song "Squeeze the Trigger," I'm giving the first authentic view of *my* city—not Malibu mansions and pool parties in Beverly Hills. This was the flip side to all the glamour people saw in David Lee Roth's "California Girls," which at the time was a big hit on MTV. As crazy as it sounds now, when I made that album, a lot of people didn't even realize L.A. had gangs!

Murder, intrigue, somebody must bleed
Miami Vice is small-time, L.A.'s the big league
From the Rollin' 60s to the Nickerson G's
Pueblos, Grape Street, this is what I see
The Jungle, the 30s, the V.N.G.
Life in L.A. ain't no cup of tea

I had to try to represent the whole of L.A.'s gang culture. I had to be very strategic so I wouldn't have beef. In that verse I made sure to bounce between Crip and Blood neighborhoods to keep a balance. That's why I shout out Rollin' 60s and Nickerson Gardens—Crip set and Blood set. The Jungle and the 30s—Blood set and Crip set.

It was a calculated risk, but I needed to take it if I wanted the record to be authentic and reflect our lives.

On that first album, I'm not trying to go toe to toe lyrically with the New York heavyweights like Melle Mel or Grandmaster Caz. But I already had enough confidence to know that my content was unique. My delivery was unique.

More than any other rapper out there, I was willing to push the envelope. I had my pimpin' raps, my sex raps, my super-violent crime raps. I rapped about Reagan and Iran-Contra, about racism and police brutality. I was using more profanity than any rapper had before. That's why *Rhyme Pays* was the first album to get slapped with a Parental Advisory warning sticker for explicit language.

When I found out, I said, "Good! I don't give a fuck!"

I was trying to be the edgiest, hardest-sounding, most thought-provoking rapper in the game.

In fact, because my image was so based on crime and violence, that was the main question people had about me: Could an artist build an entire career on sounding so dark and negative?

CHAPTER 4

THE SYNDICATE

My life is violent
But violent is life
Peace is a dream
Reality is a knife

—ICE, "COLORS"

SPIKE

For most of 1986, while Ice was off in New York getting his deal and recording *Rhyme Pays*, I was trying to get my cocaine hustle on. I didn't have a long run in that game—only lasted seven months before I got knocked.

The first thing I did was recruit some young homies from the 30s to sell the dope for me. My daughter's mother lives in Bakersfield—so I'm out there a lot anyway visiting her and buying her clothes and things she needs for school. Houses out there are a lot cheaper than in South Central, so I rent four places in Bakersfield. I teach these youngsters how to cook that powder into crack, set up the rock-houses, and it's selling fast, so I start to re-up with Bruce. Before long, I realize I need to expand, to start selling someplace out of state. I'd hit one successful jewel lick in Oklahoma, so I drove out there and set up a few rockhouses.

But like Ice says, selling cocaine is different than hitting jewel licks; there's too many moving parts in that drug hustle. We ended up having beef with a local guy slinging crack in Bakersfield. See, in places like Bakersfield, there's always this kind of jealousy factor if they know you're from L.A. It's like, "These L.A. niggas think they better than us." Well, maybe we do. Whatever. This dude stole $600 worth of dope off us, guns got drawn, he did a drive-by, shot up one of our rockhouses. Nobody was hit but the police showed up, started asking a bunch of questions, and I tried to tell them I was just some dude from L.A. who got lost on the highway and was asking for directions. But once they ran my license plates and found out I was fresh out on parole, an automatic hold got put on me in Bakersfield.

The prosecutor tried to hit me with a new drug felony, but I found a good defense attorney and gave him seven grand.

When we show up at court, he smiles. "I went to law school with this judge."

They go have a private conference and we get that felony dismissed. But I still had to do some time for the parole violation.

It was only going to be about a year, but I had to serve the violation way up in Susanville. That's in the northeast part of the state, the most remote prison they can send you to. When they take you on the bus to Susanville, you literally have to leave the state, cross into Nevada, go through Reno, and then dip back into this mountainous part of California. If you're an L.A. dude like me, you might as well be in fucking Alaska. Dudes used to call Susanville "Lose-Your-Girl-World" because even if you've got a good marriage, a good relationship, it's such a long-ass trip for anyone to make, almost no one got visits.

The yard in Susanville is organized into ten separate dorm buildings with about thirty bunks in each one. When I was there, Susanville was predominantly a Norteño prison—they pretty much ran the place—and the Black population was mostly Crips. Very few Bloods on that yard. I got there in February of 1987, and by May, all fucking hell broke loose between the Hispanics and the Blacks.

By this time, I wasn't the young kid learning the ropes at Soledad. I had some authority up in Susanville—me and this cat named Romeo had the keys to the 30s car.

The riot popped off on Cinco de Mayo, when the prison allowed the Norteños to have a special celebration. They'd roped off part of the yard and had a live mariachi band. The football field was packed. All the Hispanics were sitting on the grass in a circle, listening to the music.

Some of the Blacks were upset because they felt like the Mexicans were imposing their culture on everyone. The TV channels that day were all showing Mexican movies. The meals were Mexican food.

Back then, the prison system still used to allow inmates to have flags—red and blue bandannas—and right during the Cinco de Mayo concert, these three Crips from Compton tied blue rags around their heads. Without giving any of us a heads-up, just out of anger, on impulse, they lifted the ropes and crossed over to where the mariachi band was playing.

I'm on the weight pile, looking at this from a distance, saying, "Oh shit! What the fuck are these niggas doin'?"

In prison one of the first things you learn is to give different races their space.

One of these dudes is a well-known individual from Compton, six-foot-four, arms super swole—I'd been on the iron pile with him and he was a monster. He has two youngsters on either side, strolling through the circle of a few hundred Hispanics with a purpose, damn near walking right through the mariachi band. As they get into the heart of that circle, they start throwing their set up, saying, "Fuck y'all! This is Crip!"

All the Hispanics jumped to their feet. In unison. The music stopped. Somehow those Crips made it through the circle without getting attacked, but the tension was crazy. I mean, Norteños are a serious entity in prison—they are definitely with the business.

All of us on the iron pile are staring at each other. We know the Norteños can't let that go. That's the ultimate disrespect. It's level-ten disrespect. The police in the gun towers know it, too. They don't even wait thirty seconds. You immediately hear the towers giving the command:

"Yard recall!"

Next thing I'm expecting to hear is a gunshot—because a few weeks earlier, I saw one whiteboy get blown away by a guard with a Mini-14 rifle. He was trying to shank a Black dude, they shouted, "Yard recall!" the whiteboy didn't stop stabbing, and one police up in the gun tower killed him with a single shot through the chest. Left an exit wound in his back the size of a cantaloupe.

When it's a yard recall, everybody has to return to the dorms instantly. They lock us inside. We know what's fixing to go down at nightfall. We know the Hispanics are organizing their response.

One thing I learned about the Hispanics in prison: spontaneity is not their get-down. When they move, they move deliberately, like a pack of lions. And you can't underestimate nobody in their car. Could be a fifty-year-old man who sits in the corner all day reading his Spanish Bible, or a scrawny little dude who's ninety pounds soaking wet—when the shot-caller says "Go!" damn near 100 percent of them are ready to go.

What the three Crips from Compton did was foul—no question. And protocol says it's our job to DP them. Meaning, as Crips, we decide how to discipline them. It's called "in-house cleaning." We could take them into the back of a dorm and say, "Yo, you disrespected the prison politics." Depending on the situation, dudes might get hands and feet put on them, get stabbed up, rolled off the yard.

Once we get locked into the dorms, there's about an hour of suspense. In Susanville, like every other prison, the administration knows who *really* runs shit. If there's about to be a racial situation, they'll let the shot-callers talk face-to-face, in open view, while the police stand off at a distance, and maybe there'll be a resolution that avoids a full-on war.

They start opening the dorms and letting out the Black dudes with influence. It's me, my homie Romeo, one Hoover, and two dudes from 60s. No Bloods. The administration knows that this is a Crip versus Norteño situation.

We're standing in the middle of the football field, and the Norteño shot-caller comes walking out with his lieutenant. There's a very distinctive look to the Norteños. A lot of the Sureños keep their heads shaved, almost like skinheads, but the Norteños in the '80s used to have long hair, usually in ponytails or mullets.

This dude was about thirty-five, had a very proud walk, long black hair, handlebar mustache. I didn't know his name or his background, but I knew he was with the business. His lieutenant was younger, bigger, looked like a serious dude, too.

They joined us in the middle of the football field.

"What the fuck was that?" the shot-caller says. "Your people disrespected us. They gotta get off the yard!"

He put his demands on the table immediately. My homie Romeo says, "Well, wait a minute, man, we're going to holler at their people." Meaning, we'll start our process of investigation and come to a judgment. No doubt we have to DP them. But how we do it, when we do it—that's our decision, not the Norteños.

I always try to talk with respect, in the streets and in prison. But I've also always been the kind of dude who will check a bully in a minute. And I didn't like the Norteño shot-caller giving us an ultimatum. Before Romeo even finished talking, I jumped into the conversation.

"Check this out, man. First of all, we understand that you feel that somebody disrespected you. But now you're telling us what the fuck to do. You're telling us we gotta roll up our people. Don't *nobody* outside our race tell us what to do."

He's staring hard at me—I feel his energy. I know this motherfucker is *never* gonna back down.

"We know you guys ain't no punks," I tell him, "but we ain't no punks, either. We know the prison politics just like you know the prison politics. We decide how to DP our own—"

He cuts me off. "No, they *got* to go."

Now I'm getting heated.

"You want someone rolled off this fucking yard? How 'bout this then? You wanna get down with one of them? Plain and simple, you get down with one of them and loser gets rolled off this yard?"

His lieutenant to the side of him leans in close, saying, "Big homie, I'll fight whoever."

"Oh, he wants to take on the challenge? He wants to take on your fade?" I walk over to the dorms where a couple of these Compton Crips were at. "Yo, get the doors open!" I'm telling the police to let one of the Compton dudes out. But they won't open the doors.

Nothing got resolved in that meeting. Honestly, all I did was throw more gasoline on the fire. But here's the thing: their shot-caller was giving us orders to roll up our own people—and you can't let that pass in prison. *Never.* No race can tell another race how to discipline its own.

Once the guards come around to do the count at 9 p.m., locking us in the dorms, it's fixing to go down. Everyone in the entire prison knows this is about to get ugly. All ten dorms have a mixture of Blacks, whites, and Hispanics, and there's no police in there with us at night.

Those of us with the keys to our various cars send out the word—doesn't matter if you're Crip, Blood, or just a civilian.

I told my people: "If you're Black, you're fixing to get hands and feet put on you tonight. Make sure you get into bed with your boots and your weightlifting gloves on. Get you some steel, a sardine can, a sharpened toothbrush—whatever it is you need to go into battle."

We only had about six Hispanics in my dorm, and when they saw me and the homies sharpening our shit, getting ready for war, they all grabbed their belongings and asked to be let out of the building. This was happening in all the dorms; anyone who didn't want part of the fight was trying to leave. The administration was letting dozens of dudes into the programs office for their own safety.

When it comes to race wars in prison, I've learned one thing: size don't mean shit. Some of the biggest, meanest-looking dudes will be the first to PC up—ask for protective custody. In fact, I look out the window and see this same six-foot-four Compton Crip who instigated the whole shit by walking through the Cinco de Mayo concert, this motherfucker who was big and strong enough to snatch an engine out of a car, and *he's* walking across the yard to the programs office to PC up. The same dude who said, "Fuck y'all! This is Crip!" didn't want no part of the drama and asked for ad-seg, administrative segregation.

"Ain't that some shit?" I say to Romeo.

The police do the nine o'clock count. Then, once we're all locked in for the night, some horrific shit jumps off.

Immediately, you start hearing screams from inside nearly every dorm building.

Susanville's located in a little valley surrounded by mountains and all you can hear is these echoes of screams rolling through. Guys getting stuck in the chest and gut. Guys getting their faces and throats slashed. The Norteños knocked out one Black dude, stomped him unconscious, then they took a broken broomstick and used it like a spear. Stuck him through his chest all the way through his back. He got ran through like a shish kebab.

Outside there's this white van we call the "meat wagon," taking people out to get emergency treatment all night. At least twenty people wind up getting taken away for life-threatening wounds. The dude that got impaled on the broomstick had to be airlifted off the yard by helicopter.

Police are streaming in from all kinds of other yards, wearing riot gear, using pepper spray and percussion bombs. They can't contain the war, so they make every single one of us go outside, stripped down to our boxers. They lay us flat on our stomachs with our hands behind our backs and zip ties on our wrists. It gets so cold up there in those mountains that even in May there's snow on the ground—for hours, we're lying there freezing our asses off in just our boxers until the police regain control of the yard.

The Norteños got the better of us—in terms of casualties. They had the numbers on the yard, and they had the more disciplined organization.

The saddest part was knowing that lot of Black dudes who weren't Crips—guys who weren't even gangbanging—got stabbed up and scarred for life. When a war like that jumps off, you're not only guilty by association, you're guilty simply by race.

The next day the police launched a major investigation. It went up to the highest levels in Sacramento. They moved the Norteño shot-caller off the yard. Moved a bunch of Crips, too. The whole of Susanville stayed on lockdown for five months.

We were eating in our dorms every day, no rec time, no programs, couldn't hit the weight pile. And everybody knew the drama could jump off again at any time.

The one bright spot was a few months before I'm scheduled to parole out, I get word from L.A. that Ice's debut album, *Rhyme Pays*, dropped—and even without radio play, it's a hit. Ice is putting together a new crew called the Rhyme Syndicate and he wants me to be an integral part of the team—along with Al P., Nat the Cat, Bebop Bill, Vic, Sean E. Sean, Sean E. Mac. When the national touring starts in '88, Ice says he wants me onstage with him at every show.

ICE

I always promised my friends, "If I get put on, I'll come back and put the rest of you on." That was really important to me. Solidarity. Loyalty.

My philosophy of success has always been this:

No man can be great *alone*.

You're only great when other good people hold you in high regard.

When I signed my deal with Sire and came back to L.A., the first thing I looked to do was create a new organization. It was partly to bring together young talented MCs, DJs, and producers who were trying to get into the music business. And it was partly for my player friends like Spike. I knew that lot of my dudes who were street criminals had the talent and intelligence to get out of the game. The only thing they lacked was opportunity.

When I was in New York City and hung out with the Universal Zulu Nation, that sparked the germ of an idea in me. I liked how the Zulu Nation had all these different rap groups working together under one alliance.

I wanted to bring that template back to Los Angeles. But I knew L.A. was way too gangster for something as Afrocentric as the Zulu Nation. If I wanted to create a musical alliance, I had to create my own *gang*.

No, I wasn't trying to inject L.A. gangsterism into the music business. Back then, at the time of my first album, the shit was way too real. Before the truce in 1992, gangbanging was pretty much "onsight." Meaning, if you got caught in the wrong place wearing the wrong color, they'd just shoot you.

When I was first coming out as a rapper, it wasn't a smart move—artistically or businesswise—to claim a set. Yeah, I'm friends with Rollin' 60s, but if I start claiming 60s publicly, I immediately become enemies with half the niggas in L.A, you know? Yeah, I'm friends with Harlem, but if I start claiming Harlem, I've instantly got problems with all of Harlem's enemies.

I'm in the process of trying to change occupations, you know? I'm trying to get out of these streets and into entertainment, so I'm not trying to claim a set—I'm trying to claim the *whole* of the West Coast.

While I was thinking about starting this new organization, I was reading a few books about the early days of the mob. I'd been studying up on Charles "Lucky" Luciano and how he created the Commission. It was a way of organizing the mob families not to kill each other over petty bullshit—to resolve their beefs in some structured way with formal sit-downs and certain agreed-upon rules.

And back in Luciano's day, they used to refer to the mob as "the Syndicate." The definition of a syndicate is a group of individuals combining to promote some common goal. This was exactly my theory of what we had to do with hip-hop in L.A. The Rhyme Syndicate's common goal was for all of us to be successful rappers. Now, the key to any syndicate is this: Nobody can be the boss. All the different groups have their own bosses, but we agree to sit down and talk before we take each other's heads off.

Most of my friends from L.A. are Crips—meaning, like Spike, they grew up in Crip neighborhoods, but my homie Randy Mac is from V.N.G.—he's Van Ness Gangster Brims. We've known him since he was a kid and that was never an issue: Randy Mac was still 100 percent Rhyme Syndicate. We made it real clear—no blue and red, no cuz and blood, in the recording studio or on tour. No gangbanging, period—not if you wanted to be down with the Syndicate. To me, the Syndicate was about building *unity* with all of L.A.'s dopest rappers, DJs, and producers—regardless of what neighborhoods they were from.

Inside the Syndicate, we had a lot of talent. Evil E, Hen Gee, DJ Aladdin, Everlast, WC, Donald D, Toddy Tee. By 1988, Afrika Islam and I had gotten a deal with Warner Bros. to do a compilation album called *Rhyme Syndicate Comin' Through*. We had some of the most talented West Coast artists with us, like Low Profile—that's WC and

DJ Aladdin—as well East Coast lyrical beasts, like Donald D from the Bronx and Divine Styler from Brooklyn.

A lot of these artists were already the finished product. Maybe they needed a bit of guidance and mentoring. Take Everlast. When he was brought to me by this guy Bilal Bashir, I thought Everlast was already a great rapper, but the problem was he sounded just like Rakim. He was this young charismatic white kid from L.A. but he was using Rakim's voice. I said, "Dude, you're dope—but you're doing Rakim. All you need to do is rap in your own voice." Once he started to rap as himself, it all fell into place—we got him a deal with Warner Bros., and later on he had a monster career both with House of Pain and as a solo artist. Same with Donald D and Divine Styler— I was able to get them signed as solo artists as well.

On top of these artists who were ready on day one to start recording and doing shows, I had my street dudes waiting in the wings. The cats I'd been hustling with were all eager to get into this music game. Nat the Cat, Spike, Sean E. Mac, they were all starting to rap.

Everybody saw that hip-hop could be another lane. See, that's the cool thing about making the music business your legit career. It wasn't like, "Yo, Ice left the game to become a fucking *architect*." I was getting legit paper from music, but I was still hanging out in the same clubs as before, wearing fly jewelry and clothes, driving foreign whips. It was a shift in career, yes, but it wasn't a shift in *lifestyle*.

For some of my friends I knew this was going to be a long, slow process of artist development, but I was still trying to bring everybody onboard with me.

I said it best in my song "Mind over Matter":

I made a promise
To my brothers in street crime
We'd get paid with the use
Of a sweet rhyme

In 1987, I already felt like I was carrying the whole of the West Coast on my shoulders, and then, around the time I was putting the Syndicate together, I got a call from Warner Bros. asking if they could use my song "Squeeze the Trigger" for a movie Dennis Hopper was directing about gangs in L.A.

I knew that if they wanted to use your record in a movie, you could ask to see a rough cut of the film first. Dennis Hopper was a great actor and director, but when I watched the movie, I was like, *Well, this shit is kind of fake, you know? The Mexicans and the Blacks ain't fighting each other like that. Not in the streets, at least. In the pen, sure—that's where shit gets racial. But I get it—the film was originally supposed to be set in Chicago and it's really told from the cops' perspective. Dennis Hopper's not trying to make a documentary.*

I asked them if they had a title song yet and they played me this funk track they got from Rick James. He's singing some crazy-ass shit: "Look at all these *colooooors!*"

"Hold up, what the fuck is this? *That's* your title song?" The track had no connection at all to the gangbanging world. Me and Islam went back in the studio. King Sun had a dope song out at the time called "Mythological Rapper." I loved King Sun's cadence on that record and I used it as an inspiration for my flow:

I am a nightmare walkin'
Psychopath talkin'
King of my jungle
Just a gangster stalkin'

Even though I never banged for a set, from the time I started at Crenshaw High, I understood the mentality. Writing that lyric, I tried to submerge myself into the mindset and motivations of a young dude who's banging for his neighborhood. Even if the movie wasn't accurate about L.A. gang life, I wanted the song to be truthful.

My song is more realistic than the movie. It holds up to this day. The video started getting lots of play on MTV—after they talked me into adding this corny-ass disclaimer. They intercut me rapping with scenes of Robert Duvall and Sean Penn from the film. The song left such a strong impression that to this day a lot of people think I acted in the movie.

We hit the road heavily for most of 1988—there were a couple of major hip-hop tours featuring all the hottest artists of that year. I was performing songs from *Rhyme Pays*, and my second album, *Power*, was about to drop. We did the Dope Jam tour in the spring and summer of 1988—besides me, it was Biz Markie, Boogie Down Productions, Doug E. Fresh, Kool Moe Dee, and Eric B. & Rakim. Then straight after that we did the Bring the Noise tour with Public Enemy, N.W.A, and EPMD.

"Colors" was always my opening song. We'd start my shows with a prop LAPD cruiser onstage and I'd be standing on the roof of the cop car surrounded by the Rhyme Syndicate, all of us throwing our fists in the air.

It was during those '88 tours that we saw the impact *Colors* was having across the country. This was the first introduction to L.A. gangs for a lot of middle-class kids. One time we were in Tennessee, and this young white dude in the crowd had on a khaki shirt that said "Rollin' 60 Crip—Colors." I was tripping—like, what the fuck does this kid know about the Rollin' 60s? Not a damn thing. But I realized that to him, it wasn't a *real* neighborhood in South Central that dudes were killing and dying for—it was just a cool-sounding affiliation. No different than wearing a shirt that says "Team Ferrari" or "Oakland Raiders." You'd see dudes in Saint Louis claiming they were Hoovers or Pirus—having zero idea these gangs are named after actual streets in Los Angeles and Compton.

For guys like Spike and Al P. and me—dudes who grew up with the life-and-death ramifications of gangbanging in L.A.—to see how Dennis Hopper's movie and my title song had made gangs kind of chic—I mean, that was a weird fucking trip. My song was the opposite of glamorization: it was a warning, a cautionary tale.

Death is my set, guess my religion.

You could see the trend building momentum during those shows in '88—this mystique about the gangs of L.A. touching something with rebellious white kids all over the country. That same year, N.W.A dropped *Straight Outta Compton*, and when Ice Cube said the line "from the *gang* called Niggas Wit Attitudes," boom—suddenly the media had a new phrase to latch on to: 1988 was the year of *gangsta rap*. N.W.A took it to stratospheric heights, and I was dubbed the godfather of the movement.

Those early tours we did, I had a small army of my homies up onstage. Like fifteen or twenty motherfuckers would hit the stage with me. When I performed "Power," I'd go into this breakdown, introducing the members of the Syndicate.

I'd always start by saying, "Give it up for Spike—he just came home from the penitentiary!"

And then, like a true player, Spike would grab his moment to shine.

SPIKE

During Ice's shows, I was always the first guy out onstage and the last guy to leave. And during "Power," Ice had this skit for me. After he'd say that I just got out of the penitentiary, right in the middle of the stage, the spotlight would zero in, all these dudes surrounding me, I'd pose a bit, then take my shirt off and throw it into the crowd. All that time on the iron pile, all the techniques I'd learned from Jamo—shit, I was built like a little pit bull. Within the Syndicate, I was known as the workout king.

Evil E is rocking the turntables and with that spotlight on me, I drop to the floor and bang out twenty-five one-arm push-ups. Real rapidly, like it ain't nothing. Got these huge rope chains and medallions hanging off my neck, jangling everywhere—the crowd would get buck-wild.

I'd jump back up and we had this cat Bango from Cleveland who'd been a fighter, he'd start shadowboxing at the other end of the stage,

throwing fast combinations. Ice has this natural instinct for showmanship. During that "Power" breakdown, there was this level of energy
you could feel surging through the crowd. It was intense, man.

My life had done a complete 180 in a few weeks. I paroled out of
Susanville in December of 1987, and just like that Ice scoops me up
and I'm part of the Rhyme Syndicate—I'm in the mix with the whole
posse on the tour bus.

I went straight from that race war and five months of fucking
lockdown at Susanville to suddenly traveling all over the country,
performing in front of tens of thousands of fans, hanging out backstage with the biggest rap stars in the business.

In 1988, we did some major tours. First was the Dope Jam, then
Bring the Noise. We'd always open up with "Colors." We'd have that
LAPD patrol car and I'd post up on one side of the stage by a huge
speaker, and Bronx Style Bob would be on the other side of me. In
the middle of the stage was Donald D and Afrika Islam, and front
and center—standing on top of the cop car—was Ice.

The gangs of L.A. will never die—
Just multiply!

Ice introduced us to the whole hip-hop world. And the more time
I spent hanging out with these artists, talking to the guys in N.W.A
and Public Enemy, the more I wanted to be in that world myself. Just
seeing Ice achieve that level of success—from bashing jewel cases
with me, making getaways on motorcycles, now he's packing arenas
with fans who know every word to every one of his rhymes, wearing

T-shirts with his face on them, waiting for him to sign his name with a Sharpie.

I started immediately practicing my own rhymes. Ice was encouraging all of us: Nat the Cat, Sean E. Mac, me, anyone who felt they could flow, he'd say, "Start getting your shit together," we could perform as opening acts, begin recording our little demos.

Being that close to the action, right there onstage in these big arenas, I started to see a real possibility for a career in music. Didn't seem like a wild fucking dream. I knew I could do more than just bang out one-arm push-ups onstage.

Originally, Nat the Cat and me were going to form a group—the plan was for us to record together as a duo. Nat already had this intricate flow—superfast, with all kinds of tongue twisters—way ahead of his time. He'd already recorded a few songs as a soloist with the Syndicate. We were starting to write rhymes together. I hadn't found my own voice yet, but I was trying to learn the craft. With the money from a jewel lick I hit, Nat the Cat and I bought some recording equipment to set up our own home studio.

See, I was still straddling the fence majorly. I was bouncing back and forth between these two worlds: crime and entertainment. When I'd be out on tour with Ice, I was strictly about the music. If we'd be in Detroit, Saint Louis, Memphis, New York—wherever we had a show—I wasn't out there looking for jewelry stores to hit. I was strictly focusing on what needed to be done for Ice and the Syndicate. After the shows, we'd have parties with all kinds of girls up in the hotel room, hanging out with the guys from N.W.A. Those were some of the best times.

But when we got back to L.A., since music wasn't bringing me a paycheck, I'd go straight back to hitting licks. I had legit options shaping up right in front of me, but I was just too impatient. If you're conditioned to robbing, stealing, taking, hustling—that's what you know how to do. Doesn't mean robbery was *all* I was capable of doing, but I was so committed and turned out to the street life, I wasn't ready to leave it behind.

It's like the book of Proverbs says, "A dog returns to its own vomit." If negativity is what you're most familiar with, that's what you'll go back to time and again.

I viewed being a jewel thief as my day job.

Being a player was my full-time career.

When Ice would call to take me on tour with the Rhyme Syndicate, it was like I was moonlighting from the game.

CHAPTER 5

HIGH ROLLERS

Best believe the gats in my promo shots ain't props

—*ICE, "MAKE THE LOOT LOOP"*

ICE

In 1989, Afrika Islam and I opened up this club called United Nations in Hollywood, right across from Grauman's Chinese Theatre. It was the first cross-platform club in L.A.: we had multiple floors, and DJs playing hip-hop, reggae, and techno. The hip-hop room was the biggest, but we had all walks of life in there. You could just vibe off whatever music you wanted to. And I was using that club to give all the dudes opportunities—if they wanted to take a shot at being rappers, they could get onstage and perform two or three songs as opening acts. They could also work as security. I was trying to give them another way to hustle, make some legit paper.

It was at United Nations that I had this talk with all of them—all the dudes within the Rhyme Syndicate who'd been in the streets with me. They had these customized jackets made up—black silk with gold embroidery: "Old Crime Crew." They came up with that idea. Like, "We're Ice's guys from that previous phase of his life." I mean, before I decided to go legit with the music business, we were simply *the* Crime Crew. Nothing "old" about it.

I had artists in the Rhyme Syndicate like Donald D and Everlast who were straight-up MCs, not hustlers, but then I had dudes like Spike, Nat the Cat, Sean E. Sean, Al Patrome—all of them had been part of my criminal life, so they had a clique within the clique.

Everyone remembers this conversation now as this turning-point moment where I basically made it clear that I was out of the game. At the time, I didn't plan to make some kind of announcement—we were just having a meeting about Rhyme Syndicate business and the operation of the club and I told everybody what my mindset was.

It wasn't something I'd decided overnight. It was a progression, a series of steps that led up to that decision. From the time I made my first recording in 1983, I was already telling cats like Spike, "Nah, I ain't hitting that lick." I was already sliding away from it. Then, after nearly losing my life in the car crash, I really couldn't do licks the way we used to, running full sprints and doing obstacle-course-type getaways. But I still had the slick mentality of a hustler.

For a while, I did try to have it both ways—keep one foot in the entertainment business and one in the criminal life. But there was this one day when I went out to steal a part for my Porsche—that was when I realized that I was *done.* I was finished breaking the law.

I needed a part for my car's convertible roof mechanism. It only cost about five hundred bucks but—street hustler's mentality—I didn't want to fucking pay for it. Some of my homies had stolen a Porsche and they were supposed to bring me the part, but it was taking too fucking long. Finally, I said, "Yo, tell me where the boosted Porsche is parked and I'll go steal the part myself."

I went on this solo mission. The car was in the parking structure of an apartment building. It had a canvas tarp over it. I got the ratchet in my waistband and I was focused.

I make a beeline straight for the Porsche, peel off the canvas tarp, pull my ratchet out, and suddenly I hear screaming. I whirl around and there's a bunch of kids pointing at me from the apartment building, shouting so fucking loud it startled me. A few are coming outside, running toward me. My first thought is that they spotted me, someone's about call the cops, and I need to get the fuck out of there. But as they run up closer, I see paper and pens in their hands.

"Ice-T! Ice-T!"

Autographs.

"Yo, sign this, Ice!"

I had the ratchet in my hand, I wasn't even *thinking* of myself as the rapper Ice-T—I was back in the zone of my criminal persona, Crazy Tray.

After I released my first album, *Rhyme Pays*, my face was recognizable enough that somebody had spotted me lifting the tarp just as I pulled out my ratchet. Now I'm inside this Porsche on the verge of stealing this part—cold busted—and I just play it cool, like: "What's up, lil' homie? Want me to sign that?"

Before I could even blink, a bunch of their parents are running outside. And they all want autographs, too. Nobody suspected I'd been in the middle of trying to rip off a car part. I guess all the residents of the building naturally assumed it was my own Porsche.

I realized, *I can't do this anymore. I'm too famous to steal.*

One thing a criminal has to his advantage is anonymity. Infamy does *not* go hand in hand with fame. They're two polar-opposite things. You really cannot be a successful *and* famous criminal. It's the downfall for mob guys like Al Capone or John Gotti: they want to become famous, on the covers of magazines; real hard-core gangsters know that their place is supposed to be in the shadows.

If people know your real name, if they know your face and whereabouts, you can't do dirt and then slide back into the crevasses of anonymity. I couldn't keep going on licks when I had my face on albums in stores, with videos on TV, with my name on posters all over the country—that would have been fucking ludicrous.

If the cops were looking to find me, they wouldn't have to do a bunch of legwork. All they'd have to do is look at some flyer: "There's Ice-T—he's going to be performing on Saturday night at the Joe Louis Arena in Detroit."

When we were having this business meeting at United Nations, I told them, basically, "I'm out." Now that I had a little touch of fame, a bit of a public image—whatever you want to call it—I couldn't be doing the things I used to do with them. I didn't make it super explicit. Didn't have to. They all knew what I was talking about without me spelling it out.

The bigger point I was making wasn't just talking about my behavior. It was about the risks of *information.*

"Y'all can't say nothin' to me or around me that I don't need to hear. Y'all gotta pretend every conversation you have with me is bugged. Any of the outside shit you're doing, don't talk about it around me. Because if the feds ever ask me something, I want to be able to pass a polygraph, you dig?"

I looked around the room at all these dudes I'd done crimes with—Spike, Nat the Cat, Al Patrome, Sean E. Sean, Sean E. Mac.

"It's all love," I said. "I'm not trying to tell y'all how to handle your business, I'm just telling you how I'm about to handle *mine.*"

I made my statement and a few of them said, "Okay." A few said, "I hear you, Ice." Nobody could feel like I was selling out, because they all knew I wasn't making the kind of money rapping I used to make in the streets. In fact, by walking away from the game, for the first two years I was pretty much broke, though I still dressed fly, still had my jewelry and my Porsche, still carried myself like a player.

But my career was building a little momentum: I was doing shows, selling some records, getting legit money. I knew that for a dude like Spike, who could hit a jewelry lick for a few hundred grand, that temptation wasn't going to suddenly disappear.

When you start to come up in the music business, you have a group of people around you that are talented and you're trying to help them break. As time went on, I realized how hard a path it is to follow. Success in the entertainment industry isn't based on talent or hard work. It takes both, but also a lot of it is timing and luck—simply being in the right place at the right time.

A lot of it was difficult—psychologically. It required a kind of mental reset, coming from the freewheeling life of a player. You want to be a recording artist or an actor? Well, you've got to be able to hit your marks. You've got to be on time. You've got to do your interviews. I mean, people see the glamour, but you're in show *business*—and it requires you to do a lot of things in a businesslike manner.

A player operates on his own clock. I knew a lot of my friends might not be able to pull it off. Some of them liked to get high, they liked to party till dawn. They damn sure didn't like to take orders.

A lot of the early tours I went on, I didn't make a dollar because I burned up all my money by bringing them along, putting them onstage. Some of them, like Nat the Cat, were already recording with me, but none of them had fan bases yet.

Remember, during this era in hip-hop, no one really knew how long a run we were going to have. It wasn't this established billion-dollar industry, so I'm sure some of my friends were thinking, *Well, Ice is making this music money now, but it might last a year or two, and then he'll be back in the streets.*

Beyond my accepting the fact that infamy and fame don't go hand in hand, there was another thought in my brain. I remembered my father used to tell me that whatever you choose to do, be a professional.

I took that to mean, if you're going to be in the underworld, then do that. Full-time. Professionally. That's your career: you're a player, a hustler, a thief. On the other hand, if you're going to be a square and work a legit job, then that's what you do. Either way, go all in. Don't straddle the fucking fence. That's how you're going to go under.

❀   ❀   ❀

Of course, I hadn't stopped representing the criminal lifestyle in my music. Ever since "6 'N the Mornin'" I'd been recording what I called "reality rap"—no one was using that term *gangsta rap* yet. It wasn't reality for everyone; it was reflecting the lives of me and my homeboys in South Central.

I made a conscious decision to show both the A side and the B side of the game. That's the influence of reading Iceberg Slim's books. Sure, I'm going to show you the glamour and fast money that entice cats to want to be players, but also how they end up getting shot, overdosing, doing life in prison. There are no success stories among gangsters and players unless, like me, they manage to get out in time. No one's invincible. You stay in the game long enough and you *will* go to prison or get killed.

Even though I wasn't out there breaking the law anymore, if you watch some of my earliest videos, you'll see some *authentic* players. Nothing staged about it. It's almost like documentary footage of the criminal life.

The best example of that is the video we shot for "High Rollers" from my second album, *Power*, in 1988.

Speed of life: fast
It's like walking barefoot over broken glass
It's like jumping rope on a razor blade
All lightning-quick decisions are made
Lifestyle plush, females rush
This high-profile personality who earns his pay illegally
Professional liar

Schoolboys admire
Young girls desire
Very few live to retire

Everything in that video was real. Those were our girls, our cars, our money, our guns. I made a bunch of phone calls and all my friends came strapped. The film crew was shitting themselves because they had never seen AR-15s, Uzis, pistols, bulletproof vests. It was crazy.

The thing about is, I didn't realize you could lie. I didn't know you could fake shit—not in hip-hop. To me, coming from that hustler's lifestyle, it was like: Why would you hire models for your video, chicks you don't even know? Cars that you don't actually own? I thought—naively, I guess—that if you were perpetrating a fraudulent image in your videos or stage shows, you'd get checked for it. Years later, it became commonplace for a generation of "studio gangsters." But none of that shit was even on our radar when we made "High Rollers."

Spike had come home from prison recently and he's in the video, walking though one of the shots, toting an Uzi.

In fact, that brief appearance in "High Rollers" created major problems. We were out on a national tour—the Bring the Noise tour with Public Enemy and N.W.A. Spike and the rest of the Rhyme Syndicate was with me. Spike was wanted for a jewelry lick in Arizona, and the police out there had a witness.

While we're still out on tour, my manager, Jorge Hinojosa, gets a call from the LAPD, asking a bunch of questions: "Do you know Alton Pierce?" Jorge tells them no, he doesn't know who they're talking about. They say, "We find that hard to believe, because you're standing next to him in this music video."

Jorge calls me at the hotel and says that the cops are looking for Spike. Since he was onstage with us every show, the cops could just show up at the arena and draw down on us—I mean, this situation could easily turn fucking volatile.

On the tour bus, I motioned for Spike to come over.

"Yo, man, let me holler at you real quick."

SPIKE

We were coming back from the Midwest to do a show in Phoenix when Jorge got the call about me. Ice said we needed to talk, but he did it in a fly manner, not in front of everybody. He pulls me to the side on the bus.

"Spike, check it out, man. I got a call from Jorge and the cops are asking him about you. 'Where's Alton Pierce?' They saw you in the 'High Rollers' video."

I'm not in that video for long, but I was on-screen long enough for them to ID me. I was carrying an Uzi, wearing this humungous gold plate medallion on my neck—I mean, I was easy enough to ID.

I looked at Ice. "Don't even trip. We'll part ways in Phoenix. I'll jump off the tour and go handle this."

I wasn't sure *how* I was gonna handle it, but I knew I had to step away from Ice. He made it crystal clear that he was living a legit life now, and the last thing I ever wanted was to get him caught up in some dirt I was doing on my own. After the show in Phoenix, I caught a Greyhound and got back to L.A. As soon as I hit the streets, I'm hearing that there's a fucking task force looking for me, kicking in people's front doors—my family, my friends. I don't know all the details yet, but I know for sure that I've got to go underground—stay on the run for as long as I can.

Turns out, this task force was looking for me for a jewelry lick I'd hit in Arizona with my cousin Rich and another young homie called Clint, the brother of one of Rich's ex-girlfriends. That wasn't his real name—he picked up the street name "Clint" because he was so calm and cold with his gunplay, like a lot of Clint Eastwood's characters in the movies. The three of us hit a jewelry lick and got away with a good score—mostly Rolexes, diamond bracelets, and some other high-end pieces. The police out there in Arizona ended up tracking down one of the cars we'd used, and it led them to a white kid Rich knew out there—he wasn't really part of the robbery, but he'd driven us during the getaway, and he knew who we were. They connected the dots. Under pressure, he started talking. He was able to tell the cops my cousin's real name. They contacted LAPD, who had a file on me as a career jewel thief.

I immediately moved my Mercedes and hid it under a car cover. I took my black Trans Am and got it painted bright red.

I had a bunch of cash stashed over at my parents' house and I figured I'd need the paper if I had to stay underground for a while. I drive over there with Rich, but when we get to the house, the place is surrounded by a bunch of suspicious-looking cars—

I'm pretty sure they're cops in unmarked vehicles doing surveillance.

I decide to take the chance that they may not recognize my Trans Am, since it's painted red. I pull into the driveway and then into the backyard quickly. I'm in the house less than a minute to grab the money, then I jump back in the Trans Am and we're out of there before any of these cops can figure out who I am or block my exit.

I immediately stop at the phone booth to call back to my parents' house. My sister answers.

"What's all that fucking noise?"

"The police just kicked the door in, Spike!"

"Damn, I just left there thirty seconds ago."

"They're asking for you—"

I hear a cop asking, "Who's that on the phone?" and she hangs up on me.

I tell Rich the cops are busting into my parents' house and we need to keep on the fucking move. We're on our way to Rich's mother's house to get some of his things, but when he phones her, the cops are kicking in the door there as well.

I get us a couple rooms at the Mustang Motel on Western Avenue. Me and Rich plan to stay on the run for as long as we can. I have my girl in Bakersfield—the mother of my daughter—come down and get the Trans Am before the cops can spot it.

This LAPD task force was well-known to us. It was headed up by a detective who specialized in catching dudes that rob banks, armored trucks, and jewelry stores. They'd recently killed one of my player friends who was a fugitive—they were on his tail, he jumped out of the car and tried to make it to the front door, and they shot him dead in his driveway.

Next thing I've got to do is scoop up the young homie Clint, but before I can get him, the police raid his mother's house, catch him by surprise when he's sleeping, and he doesn't even have the chance to hit the back door. The task force cops draw down on him. Within about two hours of being arrested, Clint's cuffed and in leg shackles, on a Cessna, being extradited to Arizona.

His family gets me on the phone and they're freaking out. His mother's crying, his sister is shouting at me, "My brother's in jail! Somebody's got to do something! Somebody is snitching on him and they're going to give my brother a hundred years!"

This shit is like a runaway train—Clint's family is frantic. I tell Clint's mom and sister to calm down—I don't need them doing anything drastic.

"Look, I already got a solution to all this mess," I say. "Don't trip, I'll handle it."

My cousin was the only one I told about my plan.

"Rich, there's no other option: I got to go back to Arizona and get this motherfucking witness."

So that's what I did. I drove out to Arizona alone and went to the dude's address and picked him up. I just told him, "Let's go for a drive," and before he knew it, we were in California.

We were all holed up at the Mustang Motel. I kept him there for like a week and a half, drilling him. "Look, I know you told the police everything, but this is what's going to happen: You're going to go back and you're going to have amnesia, you dig? When you get back there, you're going to say you don't know a goddamned thing. You don't know any of our names."

Throughout those ten days, I had a few of my street partners from the 30s coming through. This kid saw guns, he saw all this Los Angeles gangster environment, and it scared the dog shit out of him.

"All right," he says, "I'm going to go back to Arizona and tell them I don't know anything."

"That's right," I said. "They can't do nothing to you but hit you with contempt of court. Maybe they'll give thirty days in jail. They're not going to pin the robbery on you, because they know you didn't do it. You're just gonna have to bite the bullet, man. You're the one who snitched, now you're the one who's gotta fix it."

At one point during this week, Ice called to check up on me. Bear in mind, I couldn't drive anywhere, my cars are all hidden, so I was depending on cats like Ice and Al Patrome for rides. I needed to get to the store, so Ice comes to get me in his Mercedes with his girl. I can't let this witness out of my sight, so I've got him with me in the back seat of Ice's Benz. Ice is in the dark about the whole situation. He knows I'm on the run with Rich, but he had no idea I was going to see the witness.

"Look, this shit is not going to be a problem," I say. "I got the motherfucking witness right here."

Ice looks at me in the rearview mirror.

"What the fuck, Spike?"

If I had to do it all over again, I wouldn't have compromised Ice by putting the witness into his car. At the time, I was just in survival mode, running through money like crazy paying for these hotel rooms and food and clothes. All my thoughts were focused on figuring out my next move.

I immediately got the witness back to Arizona. When it comes time for him to go to court against Clint, he sticks to the script, does everything according to plan. The dude has a sudden case of amnesia on the stand. The DA is furious, pointing at Clint: "Didn't you previously identify the defendant?" And the witness says, "No, I've never seen him before."

Without the witness ID, they didn't have a case anymore. They dismissed the charges against Clint and he came home. I told Ice I was going to go out to Arizona and surrender. "They threw the case out against Clint; now me and my cousin can turn ourselves in—they don't have shit against us."

Even after I was in jail in Arizona, this task force kept hunting me. They were following Al Patrome around. We look a lot alike, but Trome's taller and a few years older. Al Patrome is one of the most loyal cats out there, one of the few dudes who still lives by the code. To me, he's the ultimate player. "I ain't no motherfucking gangster," he'll say. "I'm an international jewel thief and I walk through walls."

Later on, Trome told me everything that went down while I was in Arizona. He says, "Man, police on a nigga's trail—they kicked in the door thinking I was you."

The task force followed Al Patrome to this party filled with players in Beverly Hills, kicked the door in, laid everyone down with guns, shouting, "Where's Alton Pierce?" At first, nobody would tell the cops shit. They stuck to the players' code of silence. The detectives had a book of jewel thieves in the Los Angeles area and they showed Trome my picture. "You don't know Alton Pierce, aka Spike?"

Not only were they pressing Al Patrome, they were accusing Ice of being involved somehow. "We've seen Alton Pierce in these music videos. Does Ice-T have something to do with this? Is he hiding Pierce?"

Finally, Trome tells them, "Look, Ice don't have *shit* to do with any of this. Matter of fact, Ice told Spike to turn himself in."

"What are you talking about?"

"Spike's locked up in Arizona right now."

"Bullshit." They turn around and call the police in Arizona and ask them to run my name. "Have you got an Alton Pierce in custody out there?"

And when they found out it was true, these task force cops were fuming. They were hotter than a motherfucker. Luckily, I was two steps ahead of them.

Ice didn't tell me to turn myself in. That's not how Ice gets down. Fact is, Ice knew nothing about the Arizona robbery or how I was planning to beat the case. But that was Al Patrome's way of telling the cops, "Look, Ice is living his life legitimately as an entertainer, strictly making music and touring. He isn't out there stealing jewels or breaking the law in any way, shape, or form."

The witness stuck to the plan, didn't ID us, and we beat the case—me and my cousin Rich both walked, just like Clint.

When I got back to L.A., it was a reality check. Since the cops had located me through the "High Rollers" video and knew I was onstage doing shows as part of Rhyme Syndicate, they naturally assumed Ice was still my crime partner. It wasn't the last time they'd accuse Ice of being part of something illegal that he had absolutely no knowledge of. He was simply loyal to his friends and trying to bring us along on his journey.

I fully understood what Ice's intentions were when he had that talk with the Old Crime Crew at the United Nations club. Even though he wasn't making serious money in the early days of his rap career, he'd gotten a glimpse of what was possible in the future. Win, lose, or draw, he was walking the straight and narrow. Not only was he out of the game, but for those of us who were still active, still out there doing dirt, we couldn't even *whisper* shit around him. He was just too high-profile. Like he said, we needed to pretend that all our conversations with him were bugged.

Looking back on it today, I can see that Ice was giving us legit options, encouraging us to make smarter choices with our lives, challenging us to make a positive change. The ball was in our court. It was up to us to decide whether we were ready to accept that challenge or not.

CHAPTER 6

NEW JACK HUSTLER

Here I come, so you better break north
As I stride, my gold chains glide back and forth
I care nothing 'bout you, and that's evident
All I love's my dope and dead presidents

— ICE, "NEW JACK HUSTLER"

ICE

My friend Chuck D once said, "Ice-T is the only person who does things that completely jeopardize his career just to stay awake."

It's not that I'm trying to *jeopardize* my career, but once I feel like something's too easy, I always get the urge to switch lanes.

When I did the song "I'm Your Pusher," it was one of the first rap records with a singing hook—we got my friend Pimpin' Rex to sing the chorus of Curtis Mayfield's "Pusherman." It got some radio play—the song charted, and I was like, "This is too easy. Are people feeling this joint because of my lyrics or because of Curtis Mayfield?" I've never used another singing hook on any of my rap records.

That may be a carryover from the constant adrenaline rush of the game. I'm fueled by taking risks; I like an artistic challenge, testing my limits, trying something new.

By 1990, I had three rap albums under my belt, two of them gold, one platinum. I was already planning on forming a metal band with some of my closest friends from high school, and then suddenly, out of the clear blue, I get offered the chance to star in a feature film.

Before this, I never once thought about acting. No rapper had done it before. I'm not talking about the little cameo I had in *Breakin'*, or movies like *Tougher Than Leather*, where Run-DMC played themselves. No hip-hop artist had ever been cast in a proper acting role, probably because no serious director had ever thought a rapper could pull it off.

As players, guys like me and Spike and Al P. and Nat the Cat were always acting to some extent—and some of our licks definitely unfolded like scenes from movies. But that's *way* different than being on location at six in the morning, having your lines memorized, hitting your marks, and working with trained actors and a crew surrounding you, *depending* on you to deliver the goods.

I got my first starring role unexpectedly, simply because I was talking shit to some dude in the bathroom of a club in L.A.

"Yeah, the problem is, nigga, if they could put me under a microscope and find one molecule in my DNA that gave a fuck, then maybe they could angle me, ya dig? But they can't angle me because I don't give a *fuck* about these motherfuckers!"

I was in one of the stalls, and Mario Van Peebles overhead me and told himself, *Okay, whoever said that is going to star in my next movie.* He already had the script for *New Jack City* and was in the process of casting. He came and found me at the other end of the club where I was talking to some chicks—campaigning, as we say.

"Ice, I've got a movie role for you."

I'm like, "Yeah, okay, cool." I figured Mario was doing his own campaigning, you know, trying to impress these females. *We should work together*—that's a classic Hollywood bullshit line.

I introduced him to these girls, figuring that was that, but he says, "I'm serious, Ice," and he hands me his business card. "Call me at Warner Bros. tomorrow. If you're interested, we'll get you the script to look at."

The next day I called Warner Bros., and it was on the up-and-up. I drove over to the lot, sat down in Mario's office, and he handed me the script.

"What's the character's name?"

"Scotty Appleton."

Flipping through the pages, I immediately saw a lot of fucking dialogue.

"Yo, Mario, there's lines on every page. This is a starring role. I've never acted before. I can't do this."

"Sure, you can."

"Who else you got for the picture?"

"We got Wesley Snipes, Chris Rock. . . ."

Wesley and Chris are big names now, but at the time they were not bankable stars. Wesley had only done one film, *Major League,* and Chris was known for being a young cast member on *Saturday Night Live.*

I read Scotty Appleton's opening scenes. "Wait, hold up? Mario, you want me to play a fucking cop? And he's got dreadlocks?" At the time, I was still rocking a perm.

Nah, nah, nah. This ain't happening. Me? Playing the fucking police?

I left Mario's office, telling him I'd think about it.

At the time, I thought it was crazy, but Mario's idea was ingenious if you stop and think about it: find an actual street motherfucker, a guy who spent years breaking the law, to play a detective. It's the ultimate casting against type. Later, this was the same thinking Dick Wolf had in offering me the role of Fin on *Law & Order: SVU.* If you have a street dude playing police, it gives you a whole different energy—a different swag.

I'm usually pretty self-assured and make decisions quickly. But *New Jack City* had me confused like a motherfucker. How could I take the role of a cop when I'd spent so many years in the game? One by one, I asked my old crimies like Al P., Spike, Sean E. Sean, and Nat the Cat.

"Yo, I got offered this big movie role. But here's the thing: they want me to play a pig."

"Word?" Then, after a pause, they all said the exact same thing. "Ice, could I be in the movie?"

Next, I checked with the homies who were stuck inside. At this time, I was getting almost a phone call a day from the joint. "Dude, I got an offer to be in a movie, but they want me to play a cop—how you feel about that?"

Again, after a pause, I'd always get the same response: "Ice, if I was out, you think I could be in the movie?"

Ice and Spike in Beverly Hills for Ice's sixty-second birthday, in 2020.

Spike's brother Robert, influential in the Rollin' 30s neighborhood (1978–81), was a master burglar. Pictured here in front of the fountain at Tiffany in Beverly Hills in 1995.

T-Money Bonaventure, Spike's homie who was swapping cars with Nat the Cat on the day that Ice met Spike in the early 1980s.

LEFT: Members of the Old Crime Crew, including Ice (*in front*), BJ, Spike, Sean E. Mac, Sam, and friends, in 1982. RIGHT: Nat the Cat, Bebop Bill, Ice, and Spike in 1983.

Ice and a friend in Ice's red Porsche in 1983.

Spike serving a one-year parole violation in the California State Prison in Susanville, aka "Lose-Your-Girl-World," in 1988.

Ice and Big Daddy Kane (*front row*) and Spike, Bebop Bill, Nat the Cat, and Beatmaster V (*back row*) on the Dope Jam tour.

Eazy-E holding his son with Spike, a friend, Bebop Bill, and Big Daddy Kane during the Dope Jam tour.

Spike and a friend in his dressing room while on tour in 1988.

LEFT: Ice and Spike during the Dope Jam tour. RIGHT: Spike, Al Patrome, and Ice in 1988.

Spike on tour with Ice in 1989.

Nat the Cat (*standing, with three women*) and Spike in his Trans Am in Oakland in 1989.

Spike, Magic Johnson, Nat the Cat, Al Patrome, and JB at Water the Bush nightclub on Spike's birthday in 1989.

Spike's daughter, Marquise, at about four years old.

Spike on the mic with his DJ, Phresh Cutz, and a fan at Water the Bush in 1989.

LEFT: Spike and Phresh Cutz at a photoshoot in 1990. RIGHT: Nat the Cat and Spike holding Ice's award at the Grammys in 1991.

Spike's mother, Betty Jean Pierce, in front of her house in Bakersfield in 1992.

Spike standing by his Mercedes in Los Angeles in 1992.

LEFT: Jeff, Spike's former crime partner, at a party in 1995.

ABOVE: Spike's oldest brother, Terry, aka Turk, from the Original Harlem Godfathers, with his nieces Chanel and Deshonai and his son Leon at the Burton family reunion in 1996.

ABOVE: Sean E. Mac, Keyshawn Johnson, Ice, unknown, Al Patrome, and Big Rich at the House of Blues on Sunset Boulevard, celebrating Keyshawn's first-round NFL Draft pick in 1996.

Ice and Bruce Richardson in 1996.

Body Count's original drummer and Old Crime Crew member Beatmaster V in front of his new house and cars shortly before his death in 1996.

Bruce Richardson at his nightclub the World, located in the Beverly Center.

Spike (*standing, far left*) with other inmates at Calipatria State Prison in 1998.

One of the proudest moments of Spike's life: the graduation of his daughter, Marquise (an honors student), in 2002.

Ice and Al Patrome as Ice accepted his Players Ball Award on the Las Vegas strip in 2007.

LEFT: Diamond X and Frosty Mac at Michael Carter's funeral in 2013.
RIGHT: Spike reuniting with Marquise after being granted parole in 2016.

LEFT: Marjhon, Marquel, and Marlie meeting Spike for the first time, 2016.

ABOVE: Ice, unknown, Meek Mill, Al Patrome, Lil Ice, and Spike in the dressing room at *Jimmy Kimmel Live!* in 2017.

Ice, Spike, and T.I. at *Jimmy Kimmel Live!* in 2017.

Jasmine Marquez, Spike's wife, in 2017.

ABOVE LEFT: Xzibit and Spike after a show in Chicago in 2017. RIGHT: Dave Mustaine, cofounder of Megadeth and original lead guitarist of Metallica, with Spike in Chicago in 2017.

Ice, Jasmine, Coco—holding Chanel—and Spike in Beverly Hills in 2017.

LEFT: Jonathan Davis of Korn, unknown, Ice, and Lil Ice in front of a tour bus in the South of France in 2018. RIGHT: Spike standing in front of a Rolex store in Switzerland in 2018. "No longer a jewel thief; once again my mama's son."

LEFT: Baby Chanel and Uncle Spike in 2018. RIGHT: Coco and Chanel walking past Uncle Spike onstage in 2018.

LEFT: Spike onstage with Body Count members Juan and Vince in 2018.
RIGHT: Al Patrome, Fred Durst, and Spike in Nuremberg, Germany, in 2018.

Ice, Maynard James
Keenan of Tool, and Johnny
Depp at the Wacken Open Air
festival in Germany, 2018.

Spike in front of one of the
oldest castles in Luxembourg
in 2018.

LEFT: Al Patrome and Ice on New Year's Eve in 2019.

ABOVE: Michael "Mickey" Abbot with Ice at John Boy's Rollin' 80s party at the LAX Sheraton in 2020.

Jasmine and Alton Amir Pierce-Marquez in 2020.

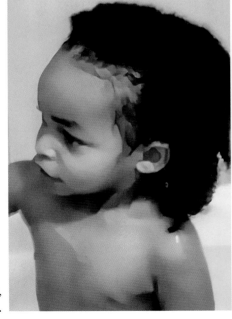

Alton Amir Pierce-Marquez, Spike's son, in 2021.

Amir next to a photo of Spike in 2021.

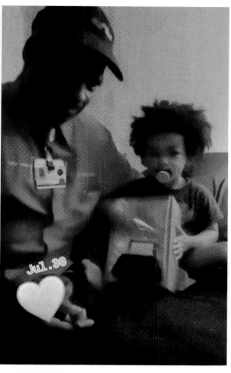

ABOVE: Spike and Amir holding Body Count's Grammy award in 2021.

Ice, B-Real and Sen Dog of Cypress Hill, and Spike at a show in Chicago in 2021.

Lil Ice, Machine Gun Kelly, Ice, Sean E. Sean, and Ernie C. at the Aftershock Festival in Sacramento in 2021.

Spike onstage with Ice during a Body Count performance at the Aftershock Festival in 2021.

Spike, Ice, and Al Patrome at the final 2021 Aftershock show— the true definition of solidarity.

The homies weren't giving me any guidance.

It was the sisters down at Good Fred's, where I would get my hair permed, who convinced me.

"Ice, baby, you better do this. You better take this opportunity to be in a movie. Y'all up here complaining about the conditions in the hood and now you got an open door. Plus, we know you're one motherfucker who's gonna keep it real. Listen, Ice, if you don't do the movie, you's a real live sucker."

I called Mario and told him, "Yeah, okay, I'm in."

But I was still unsettled. I mean, it was such a contradiction: at this time, I'm also working on my fourth album—we're calling it *O.G.: Original Gangster*—and now I'm about to play a cop?

I can't front—when I flew to New York to start shooting, it felt like I was committing career suicide.

SPIKE

Right before Ice made his move into acting, he connected me to a music producer named Johnny Rivers—everyone calls him Sleepy John—and we started working together in the studio. Me and Nat the Cat had some differences of opinion with our group project, so I went out there as a solo artist.

Johnny Rivers helped me record five of my original songs, and I started to talk to promoters to get myself little opening gigs. I'd say, "Let me just go out there and do three songs to warm this shit up for y'all." I didn't ask for money, just the chance to perform. I did a few opening-act gigs at United Nations and Water the Bush. I opened up for Digital Underground when they came to L.A. and got to hang out with Shock G and Tupac backstage.

I didn't have my rhyming skills refined yet—I had potential, but I definitely needed some direction and guidance to become more polished. I had a lot of creative energy, but it was still being misused, channeled into all the negativity of the game.

At this point, in 1990, Ice was a million miles away from the game—he was strictly doing his music and acting—and wasn't aware I was out there hitting licks. None of the Old Crime Crew knew that I was still active. After that situation with the "High Rollers" video, I was careful to keep everything compartmentalized.

In the music world, I was just an aspiring rapper. But in the game, I was a full-fledged monster. Everybody else had fallen by the wayside, had either left the life or gone to prison. I was out there alone carrying the banner.

Deep down, I didn't want to keep doing it. I wanted to go legit just like Ice. I had goals set for myself—I was going to stay in the studio, writing and recording, until I could get an album deal. But until I got signed, the only way I knew how to self-finance my recording was by hitting jewel licks. That was my exit strategy. I wanted to sock away enough of a war chest to build my own small studio in Bakersfield and record material until a label signed me.

Like Ice said, when you've been living so long as a criminal, your thinking is warped. It's upside down. As a full-time player, you justify and rationalize all your bad choices as being something you *need* to do. In your mind, robbery's not wrong—it's a necessity: *Yo, I need to get this war chest set aside so I can go legit.*

Self-confidence is a great quality to have, but my Achilles' heel in the game was *over*confidence. My thinking was constantly, *I'm not the dude that's gonna get caught. Nah, not me. Not Magic Spike.* People on the outside looking in can't understand it, but when you've gotten away more than 95 percent of the time, you start believing that you're untouchable. Yeah, I fell in 1984 and did almost four years for that lick in Ventura County, but I'd elevated my game so much since then. I'd hit so many licks and gotten away, I was feeling invincible.

Yeah, I was cocky as fuck—I mean, I saw myself as this young criminal mastermind. Looking back on it today, while Ice was off filming *New Jack City*, I saw myself directing little crime movies of my own—using actors, props, scripting everything out. The difference was, instead of doing something positive with it, I was using all this artistic energy for taking down a jewelry lick.

By 1990, the game had morphed completely from our era of finessing to the era of pistol bashes—these gangbangers pulling armed robberies had fucked it all up for the rest of us. Almost every jewelry store around L.A. had been hit so often, they'd implemented heavy security measures.

Instead of going out of state looking for places that were sleep, I started to take a closer look at licks that were sitting there right under our noses, licks we always considered out of reach. For example, there are all these high-end jewelry stores on Rodeo Drive, but players like me and Ice never tried to hit licks in Beverly Hills because the security was too high, the risk was too great. We used to say once you crossed Wilshire Boulevard, as a young Black dude, it was like you were entering a foreign country. Wilshire was the dividing line. In Beverly Hills, there was way too many police, way too much scrutiny on you.

With a lot of these high-end stores that carry Van Cleef & Arpels and estate jewelry, it's appointment only. An average Joe can't just walk in off the street. I would case the place first, looking to see if they'd open the door or talk to me through the intercom. Even if I was well-dressed, wearing a high-end diamond necklace and a Rolex, once they saw a young Black face on the video screen, they'd never let me in.

In the finesse game, we're always strategizing: *What scenarios will get them to open their doors?* I watched the entrances for hours and noticed the only people getting in without an appointment were guys in UPS or FedEx uniforms—these couriers with boxes of merchandise were getting buzzed in, no questions asked.

That gave me the solution I was looking for: all I needed was to find some white guy with an innocent-looking face to get me inside that door.

One morning I saw a UPS truck double-parked. The guy was inside making a delivery, so I popped inside the truck and grabbed the clipboard with the invoices and paperwork. Then I went down to a surplus store and bought Dickies in the exact same shade of brown as the UPS deliverymen wear. Got a shirt, pants, and a hat. Went to a popular swap meet where we were already tight with some of the seamstresses. They would embroider personalized stuff on our Old Crime Crew jackets for the Rhyme Syndicate.

I paid them to emboss the UPS logo on the shirt and hat. When they were done, you couldn't distinguish the fake UPS uniform from the real thing.

Next thing I do is go out on a mission looking for a white guy who can get past security. I'm driving around Skid Row in downtown L.A. in my Mercedes, scouting all these ragged-looked dudes, and finally I see a younger white guy, living in a cardboard box, just on the side of the freeway. I can tell he's a junkie. Long brown hair and beard. Dirty as fuck. But I can also see the diamond in the rough. If I clean him up and put him in costume, he might be able to act the part.

I call him over to my car. "Hey man, you wanna make some money?"

The only thing on his mind is getting high. I drive him out to Gardena, get us a low-budget motel room for three days. He's jonesing bad, so I go and buy him a few balloons of heroin and let him get his fix.

Once that heroin was in him and he was right in the head, he told me his name was Justin—he'd come to L.A. from the Midwest. Indiana or Ohio or someplace. Dude hadn't bathed in months. I got him showered and cleaned up, bought him a bucket of chicken and potato salad and a soda. I'm fixing to lace him and train him; Justin's my key to get through doors I can't get through as a Black dude.

After he'd showered and eaten, I took him to Supercuts. They shaved Justin's beard, gave him a cool-ass haircut—short on the sides, parted in the front. He looked like a young Robert De Niro. You'd never have guessed a few hours earlier he was a straggly homeless dude living in a box on the street. Justin was eager to make some decent money now, so he was down with the program.

By this time, I had such a reputation with my fences and various jewelers that I was getting regular tips for inside jobs. Before even trying to hit any licks in Beverly Hills, I get a tip from this one Armenian jeweler who works in the diamond district in downtown L.A. He has some kind of a financial beef with another jeweler friend of his—an Indonesian guy—and he wants to set his supposed friend up.

My tipster leaked me all this information: his friend's daily schedule and what would be inside the office. He said there'd typically be a few hundred thousand in cash and a safe full of cut diamonds. The guy worked in the office alone and kept his safe wide open most of the time.

I trained this dude Justin well in that motel room—we were just waiting for the green light. Finally, we got a call from our Armenian guy saying, "I just had lunch with him—his safe is wide open."

"Okay, dude," I said, "it's go time." Justin's job was to get inside, overpower and restrain the jeweler, call me on a flip phone, then buzz us—me and Clint—inside to clean out the safe. Inside the UPS delivery box, he had handcuffs and duct tape.

I drive him onto the block in the G-ride with Clint. Justin looks sharp in that brown UPS uniform with his clipboard and box, but he's nervous. "Look, just don't make eye contact with anyone," I said. "Don't trip off the security at the door; you look the part. No one's going to hassle you."

Justin gets past security, rides up to the fourth floor on the elevator, gets buzzed inside, and just liked I trained him, he takes the Indonesian jeweler by surprise and has him handcuffed in seconds. But before he can get duct tape on his feet, the jeweler gets up and runs to the double-door safe, rams his body into it, and slams it shut. Justin's got to improvise now. He manages to grab $120,000 in cash, which was sitting there in the drawers, throw the money in a Hefty bag, and run out. But even with handcuffs on, the jeweler manages to trip the alarm.

Me and Clint are outside the office building in the G-ride, monitoring everything like a couple of eagles. There's suddenly *whoop-whoop*ing and four LAPD cruisers pull up. All these cops jump out, guns drawn, clearing the entrance and the floor.

Justin comes to the entrance with the Hefty bag full of money but these cops don't see a robber; all they can see is this young fresh-faced white guy in a UPS uniform doing his job. They shoo him past: "Come on, sir, get out of the area immediately—there's a robbery in progress."

Justin's smart enough not to come find us in the G-ride directly. He keeps walking around the corner, then doubles back. We pull up in the G, he gets inside, and we drive away smoothly.

The lick didn't go according to script—we only got $120,000 instead of the half-a-mil of diamonds in the safe, but it let me know that the fake UPS strategy would work to get past heavy security in broad daylight. I was confident I could use the same trick to get inside these appointment-only estate jewelry stores on Rodeo Drive that we'd always considered impossible to breach.

ICE

When we started shooting *New Jack City* in April of 1990, I wasn't nervous anymore; I was fucking *scared*. Chris Rock was, too. We had a lot of heavy, dramatic scenes to pull off and we were both feeling the pressure. It got worse once we were around these serious actors like Wesley Snipes and Judd Nelson and Allen Payne. I always felt like if I messed up a line, somebody would get pissed and shout: "Can we get some *real* fucking actors in here?"

Mario and the producers had faith in us. They made it clear to me and Chris that even though we weren't trained actors, we were bringing a lot to the project—Chris was a super-hot comic on the rise, and I'd sold millions of rap records, so they were counting on us bringing our existing fan bases onboard.

The first thing I had to do on the set was lose my ego. Erase it entirely. I think that's been the key to my success overall; at various stages of my career, I've had to completely humble myself. What made *New Jack City* work is that I showed up with zero attitude. I was a wide-eyed rookie, a sponge, trying to soak it up and willing to learn from everybody. I didn't know shit about hitting marks or character motivation—all this acting terminology was brand-new to me. Over and over, I said, "I don't know what the fuck I'm doing in this scene—can you give me some advice?"

Judd Nelson really helped by taking me under his wing; he was an actor with established credibility, and if I flubbed my lines, he'd say, "Ice, everybody fucks up. Stop thinking about it so much—if you're worrying about fucking up, you're not gonna be able to do the scene. Just be yourself. Trust yourself. You got this." Judd really relaxed guys like me and Chris who hadn't been in films before.

One thing I learned on *New Jack City* is that when you're making a movie, the trick is to make it *feel* real but not *be* real. The art of filmmaking is being able to eliminate all the bullshit and repetitiveness of real life for the sake of telling a smooth, clear story.

Another thing I learned is that authenticity is achieved through some of the smallest details. And many times, those details aren't in the script.

Chris Rock often says I was an uncredited codirector on *New Jack City*. It wasn't really codirecting, but when we were shooting, I sometimes wore the hat of technical advisor for those little street details. We're making a movie about gangsters and hustlers, dope dealers and crackheads, and none of these filmmakers or actors are really from that world. A lot of times I'd step out of my own zone as Scotty Appleton and tell Wesley or Chris or Judd how shit really would get said in the game. Subtle little things like gestures and looks. Things I lived firsthand, things I witnessed, I was able to add that into the performances.

For example, that famous line I said to Wesley: "I wanna shoot you so bad my dick is hard!" Long after the movie came out, I saw cats wearing that on T-shirts, like it's an actual slogan. The line wasn't in the script; it was just something I ad-libbed in the moment. It sounded cool and crazy and believable for a street motherfucker who's fueled by vengeance.

People still stop me in the street and ask me to say that line. Just like they still walk up to Wesley and talk to him about how cold-blooded and badass Nino Brown was, or start hollering out "Pookie!" whenever they see Chris. For a relatively small movie, *New Jack City* left a big footprint—especially in the hip-hop world. Of course, we didn't think about that while we were making the film. Nobody ever thinks that their very first movie will have any longevity, let alone hold water some forty years later.

Honestly, while we were filming *New Jack City*, I never once felt like I pulled it off. I never felt at ease. When you're shooting, you start seeing yourself in the daily rushes, and the images are so raw—no music, no editing effects, scenes shot out of sequence—that you've got to imagine the potential of how this will all play out in the finished film with the magic of postproduction. A lot of times it was hard for me to watch myself in those daily rushes. I really felt I was fucking my scenes up.

After we wrapped, I thought the people I cared about the most— my homies and my hard-core fans—would say I'd made a big mistake by taking on the role of Scotty Appleton.

My feelings only changed once I got back to L.A. The first week the film was out, I went alone one night to Grauman's Chinese Theater, across from where we had our United Nations club. Bought a ticket, some popcorn, and a soda like everyone else. Lay back in the cut, incognito, in the rear of the theater behind some dudes who looked like street motherfuckers.

My first moment on-screen, sure enough, they started heckling me.

"Look at Ice in that big-ass fuckin' hat."

"He looks stupid in them dreads."

But about ten or fifteen minutes into the movie, these same dudes were shouting out:

"Don't do it, Scotty!"

"What the fuck, Scotty?"

Under my breath I started laughing. They'd stopped dissing "Ice" and were yelling at "Scotty."

That's the first time I thought, *Yo, I'm actually pulling this shit off.*

SPIKE

I t was around 10 a.m. on a sunny Tuesday when we crossed over Wilshire Boulevard into the heart of Beverly Hills. For this lick, me and Clint had two different G-rides. Justin's dressed in the UPS uniform with the clipboard, and the plan is for him to run up to the entrance of this estate jewelry store on Rodeo Drive, buzz the intercom, and say that some Black dudes roughed him up and stole his UPS truck.

I'd been through this fifty times with Justin, he had his lines down pat, but he needed to look believable, so when we pulled up to the lick, I told him, "Sorry, dude, you're gonna have to take one for the team." I didn't tell him about this wrinkle in the plan until we got there. He closed his eyes and I gave him a good sock in the mouth.

With a fresh fat lip, blood streaming through his front teeth, Justin runs up to the jewelry store and presses the intercom, saying, "These two Black guys just stole my truck!"

I know exactly how these rent-a-cops think. More than anything, they're hardwired to want to play the hero. If someone comes to them in distress, they'll almost always leave their posts to help. They're more gung-ho than actual cops.

After they see him bleeding in their video monitor, they open the door and Justin says, "Down around the corner, they're in my truck now!"

The security guys have their walkie-talkies out and they're running down the block, chasing after the supposed robbers. Back then it would take the Beverly Hills cops two or three minutes to get to the scene of a robbery. I only need twenty seconds inside the store, but I want those security guards a little farther away from the front door.

On the corner, I've got my second stage prop—she's a female member of the team—playing the part of a civilian, waving them toward her.

"They took his truck! They just went that way!"

The two security guards go sprinting down the block, round the corner, trying to get a glimpse.

Now the *real* robbers—me and my partner Clint—enter the scene. We don't even run. We just stroll in. Justin's left the door open a crack. We're wearing ski masks and gloves. We pull out the sledgehammer, bash the glass, grab the Rolexes and diamonds, throw them in the pillowcases, and we're out.

We jump in our first G-ride, a banana-yellow Dodge, drive two blocks, pull into an alleyway, and switch to a second G-ride, a white Impala. We don't give a fuck if any witnesses see us jumping into the yellow Dodge because by the time the cops start looking for us, we'll be long gone in the second G.

We rip off the ski masks and gloves. Not only do we have a switcheroo G-ride, we also have two sets of clothes on, so me and Clint strip off the outer layer. It's like a complete costume change. In that alley we ditch our outer clothes and masks and leave that banana-yellow Dodge. We make a smooth getaway in that white Impala.

A few blocks further, we rendezvous with Justin and the chick who played the innocent bystander. Everything went off like clockwork. A perfect score. I went down to one of my fences and cashed in for about $400,000 from that lick. Of course, that had to be split up between everybody on the team.

I took my entire cut and invested it in studio equipment—samplers, mixing board, reel-to-reels—so I could devote myself to my music in Bakersfield. My girlfriend's cousin was a DJ named Phresh Cutz—he'd had a local hit called "Suzuki Samurai"—and we teamed up and started to record a bunch of brand-new tracks.

I still had a magic number in my head—$1 million—and I wasn't quite there yet.

If I could get that $1 million socked away, I was ready to follow in Ice's footsteps and leave the game forever.

CHAPTER 7

BODY COUNT

Goddamn, what a brother gotta do
To get a message through
To the red, white, and blue?

—ICE, "BODY COUNT"

ICE

When we were making the *O.G.: Original Gangster* album in 1991, I decided to include the song "Body Count" by my new heavy metal band. Technically that self-titled song is our debut recording, but the origins go back a long way—back to the mid-1970s at Crenshaw High.

My interest in rock started when I first came to L.A. and was sharing a bedroom at my aunt's place in View Park with my cousin Earl. He'd already graduated from Dorsey High and thought he was Jimi Hendrix. Wore a scarf around his head, played air guitar, and only listened to KMET and KLOS—the two rock stations in L.A. He was a Black hippie. He controlled the music in the room, so at age fourteen, my mind was saturated with Hendrix, Black Sabbath, Leon

Russell, Mott the Hoople, Blue Öyster Cult, Deep Purple. I started to pick out the songs I liked. I gravitated toward the heavier stuff: Edgar Winter, Zeppelin, and Black Sabbath.

When I got to Crenshaw High, I met Ernie Cunnigan, a super-talented brother who grew up in the V.N.G. hood—and everyone called him Ernie C. Ernie was a dedicated musician; he'd walk around almost every day with his electric guitar strapped over his shoulder. He did this one concert at Crenshaw, had these home-made flash pots, played Peter Frampton licks. The audience was about a hundred and fifty kids, most of them Crips, and even if they weren't into rock, they all respected Ernie C. for his showmanship and skills.

Another of my close friends at Crenshaw was Vic Wilson—Beatmaster V—and he could play the hell out of the drums. When I first got my deal with Sire in 1986, anybody with any musical aptitude gravitated toward me. Ernie and Vic would constantly ask me about coming into the studio for my recording sessions.

"Nah, this is hip-hop," I said. "It's all based on samples and my DJ scratching. I mean, I don't really need no band."

But if you go back and check my early recordings, there's always been a hard-rock element. The opening cut on *Rhyme Pays* is built around a classic-rock riff, and I had Beatmaster V playing live drums over the sample. In 1989, on my third album, *Iceberg/Freedom of Speech . . . Just Watch What You Say!*, we did this track, "The Girl Tried to Kill Me," that rocks as hard as anything I ever did before—Ernie C. and Vic killed it in the studio. It's an Ice-T rap record, but the seeds of Body Count are already there.

Like a lot of the best things you do artistically, Body Count wasn't planned—it just happened spontaneously. We were working on the *Original Gangster* album at Sound Castle studio in Hollywood and there'd always be a ton of people dropping by my sessions. Ernie C. comes down with his guitar and Beatmaster V's already there. Once again, they're asking me about playing live on the album.

Instead of them just backing me up, I said, "Why don't we form a band? An actual metal band?"

It was just going to be a side project for Ernie C. to have a creative outlet. The rest of that original lineup was Mooseman on bass and D-Roc on rhythm guitar. Moose went to Crenshaw with us and was a beast on the bass. D-Roc was one of Ernie's young guitar students.

Our sound just fell into place: we fused the metal intensity of Black Sabbath and Slayer with some of the L.A. punk attitude of Suicidal Tendencies, and lyrically, I'm singing about the same stuff I do in my hip-hop. That blend made us unique.

We did that first song, "Body Count," and we liked the name for the band too, because it had a bunch of meanings to us. On the actual song I say, "Last weekend thirty-seven kids killed in gang warfare in my backyard," referring to the fucked-up level of violence in the hood—but another reason we went by "B.C." was the initials included both Bloods and Crips.

We went out there, playing little bars and pizza joints, not making any money, just testing out the concept. The first official Body Count show was at the Coconut Teaszer on Sunset Boulevard on April 1, 1991. We linked up with these guys Dirty Rotten Imbeciles, or D.R.I., a hardcore thrash band, and headed up to Northern California to do some gigs with them. Some skinheads in the crowd started booing us, wondering what a bunch of Black street dudes were doing gigging at a thrash-punk show. Five minutes into the set we had them slam dancing.

Right from the jump, I started to get all kinds of questions about why a bunch of Black dudes from South Central would be playing heavy metal, and I'd always say, "Look, rock 'n' roll was created by Black people—Chuck Berry, Bo Diddley, Little Richard." They took the blues, electrified it, sped it up. Even the name—*rock 'n' roll*—was just the old-time Black slang for fucking—straight up!

Rock to me is just straight-up aggression. In hip-hop, we always say, "We gonna rock the house!" or, "I'm gonna rock this mic!" You'll never hear a motherfucker say, "I'm gonna R&B this mic!"

On the *O.G.* album you hear me doing a little interlude where I say, "I feel sorry for anyone who only listens to one form of music."

As we were gigging, Ernie C. connected us with Perry Farrell from Jane's Addiction. Perry pitched me this idea of doing a cover of the Sly Stone song "Don't Call Me Nigger, Whitey" for a video they were shooting. We're staring at each other across the stage, wearing shades, going back and forth:

"Don't call me nigger, whitey."

"Don't call me whitey, nigger."

The shit was pretty out there for 1991. Then Perry started telling us about this concept he had called Lollapalooza, a traveling festival mashing together alternative, punk, heavy metal, and hip-hop acts.

It sounded fucking crazy to me, but I dig most shit that sounds fucking crazy. "Man, listen, I'm down—put Ice-T on the bill." I didn't even tell Perry my plan to introduce Body Count to the world on the tour.

The first Lollapalooza show was at the Irvine Meadows Amphitheatre on July 23, 1991. They told me, "Ice, you're going to go on third, after Butthole Surfers and the Rollins Band." An Ice-T set is normally an hour, but I decided to split it right down the middle, do thirty minutes of Ice-T material, then thirty minutes of Body Count. After I did my hip-hop set, I paused and looked out at about twenty thousand people.

"Now I'm about to prove to you that rock 'n' roll has nothing to do with color. Rock 'n' roll is a state of mind."

Then Body Count emerges. We hit them with "Cop Killer," "KKK Bitch," "Voodoo." All our hardest shit. I remember Henry Rollins standing to the side of the stage, just vibing off our aggressive energy.

When we finished that first show, I looked at Ernie, Vic, Moose, and D-Roc backstage. Every one of us looked like we'd just run ten miles, drenched in sweat. This was all so loose, without any long-range planning, without any business agenda; it was the exact opposite of what I felt while filming *New Jack City*. When I was onstage with Body Count, I didn't have any fear.

We didn't know if we'd be accepted by white rock audiences. We didn't give a fuck. We didn't know if we'd ever make an album together. We didn't give a fuck.

In the summer of 1991, Body Count was just a bunch of friends who wanted to get together, have a great time, and kick some fucking ass onstage.

SPIKE

I was at those early Body Count shows and I remember how the crowds were wilding out—that energy was on a different level. That was the first time I saw all these white kids going crazy in a mosh pit.

In 1991, we were bouncing between these two worlds—the L.A. rock scene with Body Count and the rap scene back in the hood. One day we were all at this hotel right by the airport: Body Count was on the bill with a lot of the major bands, like Guns N' Roses. A lot of us dudes from the Old Crime Crew were hanging out, and Ice says, "Come on, Spike!" Doesn't tell me where we're headed. We get in his car and drive down to Compton, where there's a rap concert going on.

Suddenly we're hanging out at the Compton Ramada with Eazy-E, King T, and DJ Quik. Dudes from heavy metal and rap didn't mix much at the time, but Ice bounced between the scenes. He started the process of breaking down that barrier—by saying, "Good music is good music—don't try to fucking pigeonhole me."

Meantime, I was working hard on my own hip-hop using a lot of rock samples in the little studio I'd built in Bakersfield. I was using this SP-1200 to sample rock guitar riffs. I always loved Zeppelin and the Stones—all those English rock bands. The best song I did was based around a sample of the Beatles' "I Want to Hold Your Hand."

The engineer that Ice and Afrika Islam hooked me up with was a guy who'd worked on some records by Tone-Lōc and Young MC. I let him hear the demo I'd done in my home studio, just using a four-track, and he said, "Shit, I can get you signed right now."

The engineer took it to the president of an indie label called Quality Records. He calls me up and tells me he'll give me a $200,000 album deal right now. "But did you clear the samples?" he says. I realize now that I was super naïve about that, but you need to remember, in the 1980s and early '90s, a lot of hip-hop records were being released without clearing the samples first. Artists would make a dope beat and worry about the legal consequences later.

Straightaway I called up Capitol Records and talked to a team of three attorneys and they basically told me, "Get the fuck outta here!" I realize now, *nobody* can sample the Beatles. It's fucking impossible. But at the time I was so young and confident, I thought, *Just make the tracks dope and we'll figure out a way later.*

Of course, when I couldn't clear the samples, that $200,000 album deal vanished. We've got to go back to the lab and remake all our beats. I'm frustrated as fuck. But since I'm still married to the game, for real, I just ping-pong back to what I know how to do best:

Getting money fast.

Right around the time of those first Body Count shows, I get a tipoff about a lick that sounds impossible. But the way I was thinking back then, as far as the game is concerned, ain't *nothing* impossible.

It was a big international gem and jewelry show at the L.A. Convention Center. The place was surrounded by L.A. County sheriff's deputies and private security guards. You've got all these diamond dealers and reps from the different watch companies flying in from

Hong Kong, Taiwan, Switzerland, Belgium—everyone's creden-
tialed, passing security checks to be at the convention.

We're talking tens of millions in diamonds and jewelry inside—
easily. L.A. County sheriff's deputies were providing escorts to some
of the cars coming in and out. Trying to hit a lick inside there would
be like trying to take down Fort Knox.

Again, I had an inside tipster. He was a jeweler based in downtown
L.A., an Asian dude originally from Hawaii, and he told me that there
would be a Rolex representative leaving the convention with a suitcase
filled with three hundred watches. My tipster was friendly with the
guy—I mean, the jewelry business can be as cutthroat as the game, boy!

This Rolex rep was traveling with no personal security because
nobody was supposed to know how many pieces he was carrying in
that suitcase.

Just like with that lick I hit in Beverly Hills with the fake UPS
uniform, I sat down and strategized a plan. With the right faces and
costumes, with the right cars and props, we might be able to do it.

I used the same principle, went down to Skid Row and scouted
three white dudes. These guys were a bit rougher than Justin—two
had done prison time, arms all tatted up, and they'd been involved
in robberies before. They all wanted to make some money fast. I got
them cleaned up, shaved, took them to Supercuts; I had my seamstresses at the swap meet make up army-green windbreakers that
said "Sheriff" in bright yellow. Got them uniform Dickies in that
same shade of green, outfitted them with holsters, flashlights—all
the accessories that made them look just like the real sheriff's deputies at the gem show.

My homie Clint was a beast with his GTA game, so he stole two nearly identical Monte Carlos. We got the actual police lights they mount on the dashboard in unmarked cars.

On the day of the lick, we had to be close enough to monitor cars coming in and out of the convention center but far enough away not to look conspicuous. We were in a parking lot nearby—me and Clint were in a black Chevy 454 truck, and our three whiteboys were wearing the fake uniforms in their Monte Carlos.

At around 4 p.m., my inside guy calls me on my flip phone, giving me the details: the Rolex rep is on his way out of the convention center now, about to drive to the airport. His rental is a brand-new blue Taurus.

He passes through the exit and we let him get a few blocks further from the convention center. We know he's heading east and we plan to stop him just before he gets on the freeway.

He's about to pull into this gas station to fill up, but right away my three guys in the Monte Carlos hit their flashing lights and pull him over. They don't even converse with this dude, just ask to see his license, then grab the suitcase, get back in their Monte Carlos, make U-turns, and flee the fucking scene.

We had a rendezvous spot about two minutes away. Ditched all our cars, switched into other G-rides, and met up at this little low-budget motel room. Our tipster was spot-on with all his info. There were more than three hundred Rolexes in the suitcase.

When I cashed out with my fence in downtown L.A., it was a hell of a score—a half-a-million-dollar lick. Each of the three white guys got $50,000 for playing the deputy sheriffs. We gave our tipster $100,000. So that left me and Clint to split up the remaining $250,000.

The wildest part was, when I settled up with our tipster, he said that the Rolex rep initially thought he got jacked by three *real* cops. The guy really believed those three whiteboys were some gangster-ass rogue cops on the prowl.

And back in the summer of 1991, with everything that was in the news at the time, it wasn't such a crazy thought.

ICE

Back in '91, when Body Count was starting out, the situation with LAPD was just out of control. Those of us who grew up in the hood had been seeing it up close for years. Back then—before everyone in the world started walking around with a movie camera in their smartphone—it used to be the stories of guys like me and Spike, our word against the word of these cops. Today, so much of it in the open—everything that happened with the Rampart Division—straight-up gangster cops, robbing banks, moonlighting as hired gunmen.

But what you saw with Rodney King in March 1991 wasn't an isolated situation; that was LAPD's get-down. If you were Black and from the hood, you knew that if they apprehended you for any reason, they might beat your ass mercilessly, choke you, shoot you—whatever they wanted to do.

The thing that made the Rodney King situation unusual is that it was captured on video. Remember, it was filmed on one of those big old-school video cameras, the kind you've got to hold on your shoulder. Very few people had them. It was unheard of for someone to videotape police brutality on just a moment's notice.

For a lot of these white cops, patrolling South Central L.A. was like *Gorillas in the Mist*. One of those cops who beat Rodney King actually used that line. The racism started from the top, with the chief of police. They made no secret about it; we'd see police cars rolling around the hood with Confederate flags on the bumper.

The LAPD used to come in and do these massive gang sweeps, and if they caught three or four people standing around on the corner, they labeled you a gang, brought you in to the L.A. Coliseum for fingerprinting and booking.

Kids who never broke the law once, dudes who were just on the football team or working at McDonald's, they would run automatically from LAPD because no one wanted to go into the system.

White people always used to say, "If you did nothing wrong, why would you run from the police?" Most young Black dudes didn't want any kind of encounter with the LAPD—you never knew how it might fucking end.

Honestly, we used to view the LAPD as this criminal regime we were living under.

This is all the background context of what happened one afternoon in 1990 when I walked into a Body Count rehearsal singing "Psycho Killer" by the Talking Heads. Beatmaster V said, "Man, we need a 'Cop Killer.'"

"What're you talking about?"

Vic told me the story about one of the homies who got shot in the back, right front of his pregnant wife, paralyzed, left in a wheel-chair—I started to think, *Well, what if somebody just got triggered by police brutality, snapped, and went after a racist cop?*

That's where the song came from. Ernie C. wrote the music; I wrote the story. It's me visualizing some guy who's had enough, gets pushed over the edge, and is out for payback. It's a fantasy—a revenge fantasy. Like Bob Marley didn't *really* shoot the sheriff, you know?

When I wrote the words, I didn't realize that cops were off-limits as artistic subject matter. They weren't off-limits in punk rock. There was already a hardcore band called Millions of Dead Cops. Black Flag had T-shirts showing a cop with a gun in his mouth.

But when the controversy blew up, they wouldn't give me credit for having the artistic ability to write a song in a first-person voice not my own, to be able to put myself into another character's perspective.

They tried to make it seem like I was advocating the murder of police officers. As if I were personally saying, "Let's go dust off some cops." At one point, they claimed the record was *responsible* for the actual killings of cops in Dallas. I told all these reporters at the time, "If you believe Ice-T is out there killing cops, then you believe David Bowie is an astronaut."

I wrote it in a persona—a fantasy character—but it was informed by all these stories from my real friends. I personally never got my ass kicked by LAPD. But so many of the homies had stories like

Vic's. I remember Spike telling us all about the first time he was ever arrested, when he was a kid in junior high—how these white cops fucked him up, nearly killed him, with complete impunity.

SPIKE

It was during the era of dipping—when I first started pickpocketing back in junior high. I was at a bus stop in downtown L.A. Everyone was crowding together in a line to get onto the bus, and I managed to dip into this Hispanic lady's purse and steal her wallet. I did it real slick and she didn't even notice. I had her wallet tucked into my waistband and was turning to get away, but another Hispanic bystander saw everything, and she starts to shout in Spanish.

The first lady looks in her purse, realizes her wallet's missing, and I take off running down the block. But when I turn the corner on Hill Street and Fifth, there's a motorcycle cop giving out a traffic ticket.

People from the bus stop are following me, yelling, "Stop him!" I sprinted into a parking lot, crawled up under these cars. The motorcycle cop is searching for me, and he's already radioed in for backup. I start hearing sirens coming from all directions.

I got up and ran down Spring Street, dashed inside this condemned building. There's a homeless guy sleeping there at the bottom of the stairwell. I almost tripped over him, woke him up, and said, "Hey, man, if somebody comes, don't say shit, all right? You didn't see me."

I'm running up all these stairs as the sirens are coming closer, and by the time I get about five flights up, I hear the police in the stairwell coming after me. Down at the bottom, I can hear the homeless guy tell them, "He ran upstairs." I get to the top, about thirteen floors up, come out of the stairwell, down this hallway of vacant offices, no furniture anywhere. I pull the lady's wallet out of my waist, grab the cash, and stash the wallet in one of the offices. I can hear the cops' footsteps echoing in the stairwell. There's nowhere left for me to hide or run. I go into one of these deserted offices, pry open the window, and jump out onto a fire escape that leads down to the back alley.

I scramble down as fast as I can—the cops inside see me from the top window and yell, "Freeze!" But I get to the bottom of the fire escape, do a hanging jump down—it's about a seven-foot drop, I land clean without twisting my ankle or anything. The minute I look up, I see a police car coming at me full speed. They slam on the brakes, doors swing open on both sides, two cops jump out and draw down on me with their guns.

"Freeze, motherfucker. Don't move."

I glance behind me and another LAPD car comes screeching at me from the other side of the alley. I'm sandwiched between two police cars with their doors wide open. All of these voices are shouting.

"Down on your knees!"

"Hands in the air!"

I drop to my knees. They come behind me and grab both wrists, then slam me on the ground face-first. I'm not resisting at all, but one cop puts his knee on my head, grinding my face into the gravel while I'm getting cuffed.

Growing up in South Central, I always heard stories about how these LAPD cops would just beat your ass, choke you out, whatever they felt like doing—but there's a big difference between hearing someone describing something traumatic that happened to *them* and actually experiencing it firsthand.

I'm yanked to my feet and see that it's four big cops now, all of them white. They slam me on top of the hood of the hot-ass car. It's summertime, about 90 degrees, and the metal of the hood is so fucking hot it burns my face. This one cop is wearing black gloves, even in the middle of summer, grabbing me by the neck, while his partner bends down to stare right into my eyes.

"Look here, nigger. When we tell you stop, you stop! You understand me? You understand me, nigger?"

I'm trying to answer, but the other one keeps putting pressure on my windpipe, smashing it down.

"I can't breathe, I can't breathe." I'm saying it real raspy and weak because I've got no air left in my lungs. Pretty soon, all I can make is a low rattling sound.

I'll never forget the hatred in this cop's blue eyes.

"You don't run from us, nigger, you got that? You don't run from us. *Understand?*"

He wants an answer from me, but he can see his fucking partner is smashing my windpipe, harder, pushing my cheek down into that burning metal of the car hood. I can't speak, can't breathe.

When you start to get dizzy from lack of oxygen, it's almost like little shocks of electricity going through your face.

I feel myself blacking out. Then something must have clicked in these cops' heads to make them look back down the other end of the alley. About forty yards away, people are starting to gather, murmuring. Nobody's yelling or anything, but they're trying to see what's going on.

The cop with the black gloves eases up his grip on my windpipe— then releases me, so I start gasping for breath.

I'm sure that's the *only* thing that saved me: the crowd gathering at the end of the alley.

"Get in the car, nigger."

They shove me in the back seat, kind of sideways. I'm fifteen, first time ever in handcuffs, first time in the back of a patrol car, and I don't know what the fuck's going on. I'm not even worried about being charged with robbery at this point, I'm not worried about my parents' reaction; now my mind is strictly on:

What if these motherfuckers drive me someplace where there are no witnesses and choke me to the point I don't ever wake up?

These cops did not give a fuck. They called me "nigger" openly, abused me openly, with no fear of any consequences.

I guess they figured they'd fucked with me enough, though, because they took me to the station, booked me, then contacted my parents. My dad was off doing his military service, so my mom had to come get me. If my dad would've been in town, he'd have whooped my ass, but not my mom. She was a really quiet Christian lady. She wasn't with the physical discipline. She would talk to you quietly, try-ing to understand what happened and why.

I'm waiting for her at the station and immediately when she walks in—this tiny, soft-spoken, God-fearing Black woman—I see the disappointment in her face.

At this time, my mother still had a lot of hopes for me. I was doing well in school, getting good grades, playing baseball—and I was the only one of my brothers who hadn't been in trouble with the law yet. My older brothers had both been to jail, and even my younger brother was giving her problems.

They gave her all the paperwork and the date for my juvenile arraignment. Mom didn't drive, so we caught the bus home, and for the first ten minutes she was reading through the police documents.

"What were you doing, Alton?"

One thing about me and my mom, I was always truthful with her. "I stole this Mexican lady's wallet," I said. "I was pickpocketing at the bus stop and then I tried to escape from the police." I told her how even after I gave up, the one cop kneeled on my head and ground my face into the gravel. How one of them smashed my windpipe until I was blacking out, and his partner was bending down, looking me in the eyes, telling me never to run away from them again, calling me "nigger" the whole time.

Hearing all this from me, at age fifteen, it broke her heart. I could see all these different emotions flashing in my mom's eyes.

Her disappointment changes quickly to worry and fear.

Then she starts praying.

She can see my face is all scraped up from the gravel, the choke marks from the cop's fingers are visible on my neck. She didn't say anything else the rest of the bus ride home. I vividly remember my mom sitting there silently on that bus, realizing how easily those cops could have killed me right there in the alley.

ICE

When I was a full-time criminal, I never hated the cops.

A real criminal never *hates* the cops. He just looks at the cops as his opponents. I knew I was breaking the law. The law told me I can't do this, but I said, "I'm gonna do it anyway." This is the game; those are the rules. If you catch me, you catch me, and I cuff up. If you can prove I did it, I go to prison.

I never hated cops; I just thought I was smarter than them.

When I wrote "Cop Killer," it wasn't addressing *all* cops. It was addressing racist, abusive, corrupt, out-of-control cops. The kind of cops that'll shoot an unarmed brother in the back. Or choke the shit out of a fifteen-year-old Black kid for having the audacity to try to run away from them.

But one thing people need to bear in mind—especially in light of George Floyd and Black Lives Matter and everything that came about in the decades after we made that record—I'm not saying, "Fuck *all* police!"

I'm saying, "Fuck police brutality!"

That's a key distinction.

Looking back on it now, thirty years later, I'm glad I sang, "Fuck police brutality!" at the time that I did. I wrote it a year before Rodney King, and the album came out two months before the L.A. riots. "Cop Killer" was a protest song. It reflects how a lot of Black people were feeling in that particular historical moment. Folks in L.A. were at the point of exploding with rage at police brutality.

Another thing people need to realize about "Cop Killer" is that Body Count was playing that song on tour for a full *year* without controversy. Nobody even seemed to notice. The shit hit the fan in '92 because that was an election year—"Cop Killer" was a ready-made target for the president, the vice president, and the NRA.

But here's the real trip about the backlash: it wasn't that "Cop Killer" was a bad song; what pissed them off is that white people *liked* it. When we played it there were thousands of white kids at our shows, wilding out in pits, shouting the words with fists in the air. If I'd made a song called "Baby Killer" or "Fireman Killer" or "Schoolteacher Killer," my own fans would have been the first to bite my fucking head off.

But cops symbolize authority, and a lot of people hate authority. To this day, anywhere we go—Germany, Italy, Brazil—the mosh pit goes craziest when we play that song. Worldwide, cops are not the most beloved public servants.

The main thing I learned about "Cop Killer" is this: when you inject white kids with Black rage—and you do it through something as seductive and persuasive as rock 'n' roll—that's dangerous. To the people in authority, that's always going to be seen as a threat.

CHAPTER 8

THE FALL

No matter how high I climbed,
Somehow I always fell
I guess a lot of players got this story to tell
No matter how cold you roll you simply cannot win
It's always fun in the beginning
But pain in the end

—ICE, "PAIN"

ICE

The biggest pitfall of being a successful criminal is that you start to believe that what you're doing is legal. At some point every criminal who's good at what they do convinces themself they're smarter than the law, that they'll always be able to outthink and outsmart the cops. And over time, a lot of the things that they put in place early on to avoid getting caught—all these rules and safety precautions—just go out the window.

It's kind of like the first time you learn how to drive a car. You've never driven before, so you've got your seat belt on, both hands on the steering wheel, checking all your mirrors and turn signals, being super cautious. Then, twenty years later, you're breaking all the rules because driving is now second nature to you. You're not wearing your belt, you're blasting your music, glancing down at your fucking phone—that's when you get in a wreck.

With crime, it's very similar. It gets easier and easier; you get more and more lax, more and more reckless.

That's what happened with Spike. When we were in the game together, we had so many rules and restrictions.

No guns on a lick.

No violence of any kind.

We're strictly players; we don't hit licks with gangbangers.

And in those final years, when he was off doing shit on his own, Spike didn't stick to the rules. He started to think he was too smart. Too ingenious. He was definitely feeling himself. He even changed his name. When I met him, he was simply "Spike," but at some point, he decided to go by "Magic Spike."

That tells you everything. In his own mind, he became *magic*.

That was his downfall.

And it's the downfall of almost all players and gangsters and hustlers.

They get away with breaking the law so many times, and the money is so good, they become intoxicated not only with the riches— they become intoxicated with *themselves*.

There is nothing like the ego of a successful criminal.

None of us knew anything about what he was into until long after the fact. He was skillful about that—keeping things compartmentalized, keeping us all in the dark. Spike was going around hitting all these intricate licks behind our backs, using dudes who had no connections to anyone in the Rhyme Syndicate.

The final—*fatal*—mistake he made was to bring in young strong-arm kids. Actual gangbangers. Gangbangers aren't cut like players. They have a different mentality. A lot of these kids who grew up banging for the neighborhood will squeeze the trigger without giving it a second thought.

SPIKE

In the spring of 1992, just before the L.A. riots, I was busy writing new rhymes, working hard with my DJ to record the tracks up in Bakersfield, still talking to promoters about getting little opening-act gigs as a solo artist.

But I was also still always keeping my eyes open for jewel licks.

Then all hell breaks loose in L.A. From April to early May, it's mayhem. South Central is burned to the ground. Chaos everywhere. Suddenly, in the midst of all this, I hear about a million-dollar lick down in San Diego. It just falls into my lap. Two jewelry stores on the same block, filled with top-quality merchandise, no security.

When I first heard about it, I could have said, "No, I'm good. Let me just stay focused, continue working on my music. Ice keeps telling me to be patient, keep recording, my time is coming."

But I allowed myself to make these bad choices—without anyone coercing me, simply seeing dollar signs, giving in to temptation. With this lick in San Diego, it was like walking down the street and finding a Ferrari with the keys in the ignition, doors open, no one's around. A crime of opportunity. I gave in to the temptation, to the selfishness, to the greed.

What made it even more tempting is that I knew I could get some other guys to hit the lick for me. I wouldn't have to personally go inside the stores.

I had all these twisted justifications in my head.

A million-dollar lick.

This will be the one that puts me over the top. I won't have to do this ever again.

After this lick, I'll cash out for good.

After this last lick, I'll strictly be doing music.

At that time, I didn't even consider the possibility of something going wrong. No one had ever been hurt on one of my licks before. I didn't stop to imagine a scenario of this becoming a huge, horrific, tragic nightmare.

By early 1992, when I wasn't staying with my daughter and her mother in Bakersfield, I was renting a little apartment in this section of L.A. called Ujima Village, and that's where I connected with this young kid named J-Smoove. He was about twenty years old, a DJ, making some moves in the music business. He saw me driving a brand-new Mercedes and a Corvette, wearing all kinds of huge jewelry, tailored clothes, and he let me know he wanted to make some money together.

Ujima Village is a Piru neighborhood. It's been torn down, but when it was standing, it was like a self-contained housing development in the center of a park. J-Smoove wasn't a Blood—in fact he told me he was a Rollin' 60s Crip from the West Side—but he was making beats for a lot of these kids who were Ujima Village Pirus and he was real popular with them.

I took J-Smoove on a few smaller licks, and he seemed solid enough.

Looking back on it now, this was the first of many bad choices that would culminate in the worst decision of my life. Bringing onboard young gang members went against our code as players. I got to know J-Smoove a little bit, but I didn't know the backgrounds of half the guys he was running with.

At this time, I was messing with this girl named Jennifer who lived in San Diego. Her father owned a shooting range down there. She told me about these two jewelry stores that had a lot of Rolexes in the display windows.

In early May 1992, a few weeks after the riots in L.A., I went down there to see her and mapped out how I was going to hit this lick—using J-Smoove's crew to do the actual bashing and taking.

The two stores were on Prospect Street in the heart of La Jolla, an affluent section in the north of San Diego. Me and Jennifer went into both stores, pretending to be shopping—I was really just casing the places, figuring out which displays to hit, which ones had diamonds and Rolexes and the most valuable pieces, and whether they had real glass or Plexiglas.

J-Smoove recruited some of his homies—altogether it was six young dudes from L.A. who came down to San Diego. I split the six of them into two different teams. I planned to have them wearing black ninja suits and ski masks so there would be no possibility of anyone identifying them later.

I realize now that the moment I should have pulled the plug on the whole operation was when they told me they needed me to get them some guns.

"What? You don't need no guns. You go in with hammers, grab the shit, you'll be out of there in thirty seconds."

But like I said, this crew that J-Smoove put together were young Pirus—straight-up gangbangers. They felt more comfortable brandishing guns. That's how they operated.

They didn't feel they could use the element of surprise, didn't have any finesse. They wanted to brandish pistols, lay everyone down before they did the smashing.

I gave them some guns: a .357 revolver and a few pistols. But I made sure I didn't give them any bullets. The guns were supposed to be "showpieces," just for waving around when they entered the stores.

The date was set for May 9, 1992. Me and Jennifer were in one hotel, and I put the six guys in a different hotel down the street from me. I briefed them the night before, drew up diagrams and maps, showed them exactly where they would find the Rolexes and the diamonds and pearls and all the various showcases. If they got everything the way I laid it out, this was easily a million-dollar lick. Possibly $1.5 million. I already got them two G-rides from L.A. After the lick, they were going to immediately abandon the G-rides, along with their ninja disguises.

We reviewed the diagrams and the getaway plan and the scheduled handoff location; then, when I felt like I'd coached them enough, I got them some takeout to eat and left.

Next morning, I pulled up at the hotel in my Benz, saying, "Y'all ready? It's time to go!" I didn't stop to do a second briefing up in the hotel room or ask, "Did anything unusual happen last night after I left you?" I just pulled up and told them, "Let's roll!"

The G-rides were already parked there at the hotel: a blue Buick and a gray Oldsmobile. They got in the cars, put on their black ninja suits, and followed me all the way there. As we approached the block with the jewelry stores, I veered off and left them.

It was around 2 p.m. on Mother's Day. While the robberies were being committed, I was a couple of blocks away in my Mercedes with Jennifer. She was at the wheel. I felt it looked less conspicuous, since she's not Black—she's Filipina. The plan was for these two crews to make their getaways, round the corner, and rendezvous with me. They'd toss the pillowcases out the window and I'd stand up in the sunroof and catch them. That way if the cops somehow followed them, they could just ditch the G-rides and run—the most important thing is they wouldn't have any stolen merchandise on them.

We're parked there, waiting, and the first G-ride drives past me at a high speed, doesn't even try to slow down to make the handoff. That was the first indication that something was wrong.

"What the fuck just happened?" I said to Jennifer.

I didn't even know all these dudes' names—I really had only fucked with J-Smoove. I figured, well, maybe whoever is driving that car is such an amateur, he's just nervous and trying to speed away and forgot about doing the tag with me.

Then the next G-ride hits the corner. And J-Smoove's in this car. They slowed down, opened the window, and threw a couple of pillowcases filled with jewelry while I'm standing up through my sunroof. I dropped the bags in the back seat and then Jennifer drove off, really calmly and slowly.

When we got back to the hotel, I tell her, "Look, that first car didn't deliver the goods. There must be a good reason. Can you go down the street and get it?" She drives over to the other hotel but comes right back with a look that tells me we've got a problem.

"You need to go over there yourself," she says. "They said they want to talk to you."

We jump in my Mercedes and drive over to the other hotel; I leave Jennifer in the car and go up to their room. The minute I walk in, I know it's a bad situation—there's six dudes in the room, everyone's sitting there quiet, a real dark vibe, just one youngster pacing along one wall, mumbling to himself. I go straight to J-Smoove.

"Hey, what happened? Why'd your guys drive right past me?"

"Listen," he says, "the young kid fucked up."

"What are you talking about?"

I mean, they're *all* young to me—I'm twenty-eight and none of them is older than twenty or twenty-one—but he glances over to the end of the room where this one kid looks *really* young; I'm guessing he's a teenager. Still muttering and pacing back and forth.

J-Smoove wasn't in the store where it happened—he was in the second jewelry store, and everything there went according to plan.

He tells me that this young kid shot somebody.

"What? What do you mean he *shot* somebody? How the fuck did he shoot someone when I didn't give you no bullets?"

Turns out that after I briefed them and left them the night before, one of them snuck out and came back with some bullets. He left the hotel and came back with whatever random shells he could find. We later found out the gun that the young kid fired didn't even have the correct caliber of bullets—he'd used .38 long shells in a .357 revolver.

Again, I knew in that moment, this was all on me—it was my fuck-up—because I wasn't managing these guys the way I should have. I knew they were young and inexperienced, and I didn't stay in the room with them overnight to monitor them.

Now I go over to talk to this kid named Darnell, a gangbanger with no experience in jewel robberies. He's just pacing the floor, repeating the same words.

"I fucked up. Man, I fucked up. I fucked up."

"Tell me what happened."

Darnell tells me that he shot a customer in the store—fired that .357 once and the guy dropped.

"Man, I fucked up, I fucked up—"

"Why?" I kept asking him. "Why? Why'd you shoot him?"

He didn't have an explanation. He gave me a panicked reason—something about the guy turning or startling him—but to this day, I can't understand it. I'll *never* be able to understand it. It was completely senseless.

I couldn't even *visualize* how this could have happened until much later, when I saw it in court—the prosecution played the surveillance videotape during my trial. When these three guys came inside, wearing their ninja suits and ski masks, they shouted, "Get down!" Immediately, like in milliseconds, Darnell fired. The victim was literally the only customer in the store. He didn't have a chance to get down, because this kid fired the .357 straightaway. Whether it was panic, adrenaline, fear—to this day, I can't say why.

I'm glancing around the hotel room, looking at all these guys' faces and assessing the situation. I know this is really bad—an innocent bystander got shot on a lick that I organized—but I don't realize how fucking bad it is yet. I immediately go into survival mode: I've got to get these guys out of San Diego and I've got to get rid of these guns.

"You guys lay down, don't move, don't do shit," I say. "Don't leave this hotel room."

Then I take the guns from them, throw them in a pillowcase, and put them in my car. I drove with Jennifer a few miles farther south, to the beachfront. I got rid of all the guns, threw the .357 into the ocean.

I went back to the hotel, got them some food. I didn't want them traveling together back to L.A., so two of them left in a car, and I took the rest of them to the bus station and got them tickets.

I had no intention of ever fucking with these individuals again. But I made sure to give J-Smoove one big lump sum of money. It was up to him how to split the money up with his crew. "This is some serious shit, man," I said. "Make sure you lay low, because they're going to be looking for all of you."

And then we parted ways. I was hiding out in Bakersfield, watching the news. Every day, religiously, I tuned into the various TV stations to see if anything was being reported.

For days there was nothing. No news about a shooting or an armed robbery in a jewelry store in San Diego. I knew the kid with the .357 panicked, but I was still holding out hope that nobody had died.

About four or five days later, they reported that a customer in Jessop & Sons jewelry store in La Jolla, a thirty-four-year-old man from San Diego, was shot in the head during an armed robbery on Mother's Day. He didn't die immediately. He was on life support for several days in the hospital, but now he'd died. It was an open murder case, and the cops were asking for information and offering a substantial reward.

"Fuck!" I shouted at the TV.

Now it hit home, how dark this was. An innocent man was dead because of a lick I'd planned. I knew I really had to go into hibernation. There was going to be a major manhunt until they solved this case. I severed my ties from everyone, planning to stay underground for as long as I could.

But once the detectives did their homework, it didn't take them too long to track me down.

It started with them reviewing the cameras from the stores; they had me and Jennifer on video in early May browsing inside both of the two jewelry stores. They located Jennifer—she had an immaculate record, had never been in trouble with the law. They arrested her, scared her; and her father, who owned the shooting range and was friends with all these San Diego cops, told her, "You better tell the police anything they want to know." She started cooperating— they looked for me in L.A. and couldn't find me, but eventually Jennifer's information led them straight to me in Bakersfield. Of course, they already had my whole criminal history and convictions as a jewel thief.

They didn't arrest me right away. They actually had me under surveillance—tapping my phones, following me—for two months. There was a huge task force made up of LAPD, San Diego police, and Bakersfield cops, plus a bunch of feds.

They knew that I wasn't actually in the stores during the crime, but they hadn't arrested any of the six guys who did the robberies, and they kept me under surveillance hoping I'd lead them to this entire crew. I wasn't meeting with anyone, wasn't planning any other licks, so I thought I was safely lying low.

Early on the morning of October 8, 1992, my world came crashing down.

That night, my daughter, Marquise, spent the night at her grandma's, something I very rarely allowed, especially knowing she had school in the morning. In hindsight, it was a blessing that she didn't have to witness the drama that was about to unfold for her parents.

Her mom and I were fast asleep upstairs, oblivious to the frenzy of activity mounting in the predawn darkness on the threshold of our doorsteps. Suddenly, the entire apartment shook with the force of an earthquake. Startled awake, I initially thought that's what it was— *We're being rocked by a quake*—not that uncommon if you grew up in Southern Cali.

But it was the task force making entry, their battering ram leveling the front door clear off its hinges.

It was barely daylight outside. Just like in Ice's song "6 'N the Mornin'," we woke to the sounds of loud voices and fast-approaching footsteps making their way upstairs to our bedroom.

"Police! Search warrant!"

I was trying to get to my feet, discombobulated, my mind and body still half asleep. My heart was racing like the engine of a Ferrari—but everything else around me was unfolding like a super-slow-motion movie.

The infrared beams from the cops' guns zeroed in on my body and head. I turned to see a team of task force members in their tactical gear, rushing through the door, shouting in unison:

"Get down!"

They grabbed us, threw us down, tackling us to the bed. I was shoved face-first into the mattress, with my arms firmly held behind my back.

The handcuffs snapped shut around my wrists.

The sound of that cold click marked the end of my life as a free man.

By now I was fully awake—like I'd drunk five cups of black coffee—and my mind was now racing as fast as my heart.

How'd they find me?

I'd stuck to the script, gone completely underground, never contacting anyone involved in the crime except Jennifer a few days after the robbery. I figured since she lived in San Diego, she might have heard the status of the person who was shot inside the store.

Five months later everything came full circle. My new reality hit me with the force of that battering ram. My lifestyle of criminality had given me a false perception of myself. I was that super-down-ass street player, that elite hustler who felt entitled to do *anything* with no regards for anyone else's rights.

I had such confidence—*false* confidence—of being invincible, believing I'd never get caught.

As I laid across the bed motionless, stunned and under arrest, my thoughts were racing; I was scheming, plotting. . . . What had happened to that once-innocent kid named Alton, the little boy with so much athletic potential who dreamed of one day becoming a professional baseball player?

Instead of playing in the major leagues, I'd become—in Ice's great phrase—"a self-made monster of the city streets." I was Magic Spike. I was invincible. I saw myself as some apex predator victimizing society. Warped beliefs had my mind so twisted that I truly believed I'd given my life to the game. My dysfunction had become my norm. Even with all the warning signs, all the red flags that I was veering completely out of control, my selfishness, narcissism, my addiction to crime—my addiction to the fast money, power, and sheer adrenaline high—wouldn't allow me to stop even if I wanted to. Thinking I was above the law, I made that decision to hit one last lick in La Jolla, which changed the trajectory of so many people's lives and scarred a community.

All those realizations, of course, came to me much later.

In the heat of the task force takedown, my hands cuffed behind me, my main thought was still:

How in the fuck did they find me?

Lying there cuffed on the bed, I felt the icy steel of the shotgun barrel pressed firmly against my right temple, then the smell of gunpowder residue seeping down the barrel burning my eyes and making it hard to see. Momentarily blinded, eyes burning, I started squinting and twisting my neck.

Suddenly, one of the cops, in a deep, clear voice, said:

"Don't move, you fuckin' murderer. Believe me, I *will* blow your fuckin' head off."

He didn't shout it; he said it as a cold plain fact. The assuredness of his voice left me no reason to doubt him. This cop wasn't to be tested.

I realized that if I accidentally sneezed, he'd have reason to blow my head off. My mind flashed back to the time when I was fifteen and those LAPD cops fucked me up on that deserted side street and started choking me unconscious for pickpocketing a woman's wallet and running from them.

This time, with that shotgun barrel pressed to my head, I was much, much closer to dying. This time, my life was on a razor's edge. In the eyes of these cops, I was a stone-cold killer, no longer my mama's son.

"Suspect apprehended!" I heard them announcing over the police radio; then they proceeded to escort me and Marquise's mom downstairs.

The scene outside was surreal: there must have been forty cops assembled, plus a district attorney and some TV cameras set up to capture the entire scene of my arrest for the local news.

The two main homicide detectives read me my Miranda rights. Then, in two police cars, we were taken to Bakersfield police station and placed in separate holding tanks. A couple of hours later, Marquise's mom was questioned and released because she honestly knew *nothing* about the crime.

I was brought into a room full of task force detectives for my interrogation—without a lawyer present. One of the first questions the lead detective asked me was:

"Did Ice-T have something to do with this?"

"What the fuck are you talking about? I don't know no fucking Ice-T!"

I denied even *knowing* Ice. They said they knew I was lying. They knew all about my touring with Ice and the Rhyme Syndicate and they'd seen me in his music videos.

"I don't know what you're talking about."

Ice knew nothing about what I was doing—no one from the Rhyme Syndicate or Body Count did—but they kept trying to drag his name into this, wanting me to link him to this case he had *nothing* to do with.

I wouldn't give them shit. I wouldn't talk to them—period.

They wanted information—names, locations—about the kids involved in the robbery and shooting. "Mr. Pierce, you can help yourself by cooperating—"

"I told you. I'm not saying shit to you guys. Let me talk to my attorney."

That's the code I grew up with. Always keep your mouth shut.

I've never snitched on anybody. Never will.

The older of the two detectives says, "Take him away. We're going to make an example of his ass."

They transferred me down to San Diego. I was held without bail, housed in this special section of the jail that was for all the high-powered, high-security cases. I didn't trust the phones down there, so I contacted nobody. The only call I made was to my daughter's mother, and I asked her to get in touch with my mom and tell her I was all right. I wasn't going to call Trome, or my cousin Rich, and I damn sure wasn't going to get in touch with Ice—not after I saw what he was going through on the TV.

One evening, right after I got to the San Diego jail, I was in the dayroom watching the TV. It was almost the first story on the national news—they were talking about Ice. "Damn, that's *Moses*!" I said to myself when I saw Charlton Heston reading the lyrics to "Cop Killer." They were talking about boycotting Time Warner. George Bush was giving a speech about it, too. Ice was coming under heavy political fire—I mean, he was being portrayed as this terrorist threat to police across the country. I guess that's why the cops kept asking me so many questions about him, trying to tie him into my case. In the eyes of these politicians and police organizations, by doing that song, Ice had become public enemy number one.

It was almost surreal to see it, but I couldn't dwell on it too much because by the time I was in San Diego, I had my life on the line.

The prosecutor announced he was seeking the death penalty against me.

I'd been to prison, of course, but I'd never come close to facing a death penalty case—so I was nervous as fuck. I knew my best shot was to get a good criminal defense attorney. There was more than $300,000 in cash they seized from my house, and I tried to get it back in a motion by saying I'd made the money doing music—but the judge said unless I could provide receipts or pay stubs to prove the money was earned legally, they were going to hold it. I had no receipts or pay stubs—instantly, that $300,000 was gone.

And without money for a private attorney, I had no other option but to take my chances with a court-appointed lawyer. His name was Victor Erickson. When he walked into the room, I was straight-forward. "You're a public defender," I said. "Why should I trust you? I mean, my life is on the line here."

What choice did I have? I ended up disclosing everything to him, in order for him to mount the best defense he could. In my mind, of course, I know I'm responsible for the robberies, for orchestrat-ing the entire crime, but I definitely—*definitely*—did not want an innocent victim to be killed. What I didn't understand at that time was this: in the eyes of the law, masterminding a robbery in which someone gets killed is considered a more serious offense than if you pulled the trigger.

At this point, the only people they've arrested are me and Jennifer—so we're not sure how strong a case the prosecution's going to be able to mount if it's solely her word. She was there during the planning of the crime, she led me to the jewelry stores, but they still didn't have the actual gang members who'd done the robbery.

Then, right before trial, they captured one of the young guys who'd done the robbery, and he started to talk; about a week or two later they had three more guys; then they finally arrested Darnell, the young guy who actually did the shooting. He had fled to Tennessee, so they postponed my trial date until they could extradite him to California.

That's when all the dominoes started falling. All these guys came forward to give depositions against me. They all said the same thing: "He led us down there. He planned the robberies. He gave us the guns. He provided the stolen cars." The trial date was set for June 1993. I was facing multiple charges: murder, conspiracy, and armed robbery. My attorney said that at trial, Jennifer was going to take the stand and testify as the prosecution's star witness against me.

At that point I knew I was going to fall.

The only question was: How hard?

ICE

By October 1992, nobody had heard from Spike in months. We didn't even know he'd been arrested. I was engulfed in the "Cop Killer" drama—the president of the United States was on TV denouncing me. So was the vice president, and Charlton Heston— the head of the NRA—and all these law-enforcement groups. The situation got real heavy for a while. They had a campaign to boycott Time Warner, and then people started sending bomb scares and credible death threats to Warner Bros. It got the point where I finally said, "Look, pull that song off the album"—I mean, I wasn't trying to jeopardize anyone's *life* at my record company to prove a point about freedom of speech and my artistic integrity.

Listen, when the president of the United States says your name in anger, you go through the deepest background check imaginable. The "Alphabet Boys" all develop files on you: FBI, DEA, ATF, IRS. I mean, the feds want to know every goddamn thing about you. They combed through my past with a fine-tooth comb. They audited my taxes twice. They tried to find out if I was actively stockpiling guns and planning an attack against cops. Some FBI guys questioned my daughter. They were asking people, "Is Ice-T some kind of radical paramilitary leader looking to start a race war?" It sounds almost crazy to say this today, but because of "Cop Killer," they started an investigation into whether I was a legitimate threat to American national security—when, truthfully, I was just a guy in a metal band making a fucking record.

Then, at some point, in the middle of this "Cop Killer" backlash, we heard Spike was caught up in a murder.

At first, I didn't know whether the story was even true or not, whether something had got twisted or lost in translation, because that isn't Spike—that's not his get-down.

Spike's a player, not a killer.

It had been almost ten years since I'd hit any licks with him, but when we rolled together, we were never violent—that was a basic rule on any lick we did together: first and foremost, don't hurt nobody.

Al P. was the first guy in our circle who had a little bit of information.

"*Spike?* A *murder?* You sure?" I asked him.

Al P. heard that a young kid on a jewel lick shot and killed somebody and that Spike wasn't the shooter, wasn't even inside the store when it happened, but he'd been implicated as the mastermind.

I didn't even know Spike was still active in the game. I didn't know if any of my friends were. Like I said, I didn't *want* to know. And I'd stuck to that rule: "Don't tell me *shit* I don't need to hear."

I could never imagine Spike masterminding a lick with violence as part of the planning.

But here's the thing: if you're messing around in the game, *anything* can happen.

Cats think they're smart enough to control everything—but there's no way to be this *magic* puppet master, always in control of every detail and every other person's actions.

If you stay active long enough, the game will always come back and bite you in the ass.

For a long time, none of us knew what was going on with Spike. He wasn't contacting any of us, and we didn't have any way of getting in touch with him.

Spike went completely off the grid.

I didn't hear from Spike—*none* of us heard from Spike—for more than three years.

SPIKE

When my trial date approached, I made a decision: I wanted to face it alone. I needed to face it alone.

I didn't want any family or friends traveling down from Los Angeles to San Diego. Especially since it was a death penalty case. I called my mother and sisters from the county jail and told them, "I don't want nobody to come down here. I don't want no family exposed to none of this."

The morning of the trial, the courtroom was packed. I was the only Black guy in the room. There were a bunch of TV cameras, because this was a very high-profile case in San Diego. The young man who was killed came from a large family—his father was a prominent attorney in San Diego. His parents, wife, brothers, and sisters were all there. The anger in the community was intense.

The coldest thing for me about the entire trial was seeing the victim's family up close. The young man's mother and father were sitting right over my shoulder. That's the thing that broke my heart. That's the moment it became human. The crime became tangible.

These were elderly people. They didn't deserve to go through all this pain. I was responsible for their child being taken from them—my actions and bad choices had destroyed their lives.

Jennifer testified in detail about me planning the robberies, and all the events that she witnessed on Mother's Day. They had all the depositions from the guys who actually did the robbery—every one of them had taken deals on the condition that none of them had to come to court and testify in person.

The jury found me guilty after just a few hours of deliberation. Guilty of first-degree murder, armed robbery, and about ten different charges.

When the foreman announced the guilty verdict, the judge sentenced me to twenty-five to life.

At the start of the trial the judge had taken the death penalty off the table.

Because I wasn't the actual shooter, he didn't want the issue of capital punishment to possibly induce the jurors to acquit me. Knowing that they have the added burden of sending a man to the death chamber—having that power of life and death in their hands—can sometimes raise conflicting emotions within that jury room. Instead, the judge wanted those twelve citizens to focus on my role as the mastermind of the crime, thus making it easier for them to convict and to hand down a sentence that would be equivalent to a death penalty.

After conviction, I was still facing what's known as the "special circumstances" phase of sentencing. The judge told the jury that even though I wasn't the shooter, if they found me guilty of being the ringleader of this crime, they would deliberate on this as a "special-circumstances murder." In California, if you're convicted of first-degree murder and certain special circumstances apply, there are only two possible penalties: death, or life without the possibility of parole.

LWOP—life without parole—means you're not coming home. *Ever.*

LWOP is another form of death. A slower form of death. Whatever digits are in your sentence—twenty-five years, thirty-five years, forty-five years—it doesn't matter. With LWOP at the end, there's a body bag waiting on you. You're dying behind that wall.

My head's reeling: I just lost the trial and I'm waiting in the holding cell as the jury is out redeliberating. They come back two hours later. The officers lead me back in to hear the decision. The courtroom is packed, but you can hear a pin drop. As the jury walks in, I'm thinking:

These twelve people have your life in their hands. You've been given twenty-five to life. At a minimum. Now they're about to decide if you're going to die in prison.

The judge asked, "Have you reached a verdict?"

My heart is pounding like a twelve-inch woofer.

The foreman announced that the vote was 7–5. I didn't understand what any of it meant. My attorney explained it was 7–5 *against* applying the special circumstances to my case. He said that unlike the trial verdict, it didn't have to be unanimous.

Tears streamed down my cheeks and I bowed my head, praying. Because now at least there's a chance—however remote—of me coming before a parole board. Someday. I didn't want to die in jail.

They led me back to the holding cell, and my attorney came to see me ten minutes later. He blew my mind by telling me that the trial wasn't over.

"Here's what's going on. The judge has me and the DA in chambers right now—the DA wants to refile on the special circumstances."

"Wait, I thought the jury deliberated? I thought we got a verdict."

He explained that there was an option for the DA to refile, basi-cally reshuffle his cards, present new evidence—maybe bring for-ward the guys who did the actual robbery to make new allegations about me, in open court, in front of the jury. And any outcome was possible. All the DA would need to do is persuade two of those jurors to switch their votes to give me LWOP.

I waited in that holding cell while they went back and forth with the negotiations. My attorney came back and asked me, "Would you be willing to take another ten?"

"*Another* ten years?"

"Yes, ten years on top of the twenty-five to life."

In other words, if I accept those added ten years, the LWOP goes away. But also, if I take the deal, there's no appealing it later on. My back was totally against the wall. We didn't have much time to decide.

"It's now or never," he says. "What do you want me to tell them?"

"Man, do whatever you got to do."

The victim's family needed to agree to the deal that the DA was offering. I waited while they talked it over privately. My attorney came back to the holding cell one last time.

"The family said they don't want to go through this anymore. They agree to the ten on top of the twenty-five."

"So I'll get thirty-five to life?"

"Thirty-five to life."

"Take the deal," I told him. "All I ask is that I have a chance to address the family in court."

They led me back inside and I got on the stand.

"I just want to let you know, I'm sorry. I take full responsibility. I never meant for this to happen." I looked directly at the victim's parents. "Your son didn't deserve to die this way, and you don't deserve to go through all this pain. Nothing I say is going to bring back your son. But I am sorry—I am sorry for the pain I've caused you."

The judge pronounced the sentence, and those words kept echoing in my head:

Thirty-five years to life.

His gavel came down and the court officers led me back to the holding cell.

As I walked out of the courtroom, my head was spinning with confusion, shock, regret.

I honestly never expected to see the free world again.

ICE

When I was in the game, I had this vision of myself running down a road—this race full of other players and hustlers—and yelling at everybody to my left and right:

"You're not gonna win! Yo, *I'm* the baddest! I'm Crazy Tray!"

But when I got to what I thought was the finish line, at the end of that hustling road, there was no *winning*—there was nothing but a steep cliff. And all the dudes who were hustling with me, one by one they kept falling off that cliff.

I managed to stop just in time—I put the brakes on, just before I went over the edge.

Now I have a different vision. I see myself as the guy who's spun around, running back up that road, against the traffic, yelling at people, but this time I'm warning them, telling them the truth about the game.

"Ain't nothin' up there but a cliff! Turn the fuck around!"

Mostly I just get smirks and slick glances. And dudes keep on running.

I understand them. I've *been* them.

Some cats just aren't ready to accept the truth.

But everyone finds out eventually.

Spike found out in his own way, in his own time: at the end of that road, there's nothing but a cliff.

CHAPTER 9

BOWELS OF THE DEVIL

Bowels of the devil
Let me tell you what that sucker eats
Its stomach's filled with my homeboys
Guts made out of steel and concrete
—ICE, "BOWELS OF THE DEVIL"

SPIKE

For the first six years of my life sentence, I was in Calipatria State Prison, a Level IV facility in the Imperial Valley. At the time, it was the most violent prison in California—hands down.

For me, Calipatria personified the hellish reality of being locked up.

You had some of the coldest and craziest guys from the streets of L.A., the type of guys you never want to see in a dark alley, and you're side by side with them every single fucking day. In that Imperial Valley, under the desert sun, it's literally an inferno. It can get up to 120 degrees. Calipatria was the first prison in the state with an electrified fence, so any dude even thinking about escape knows he'll get fried to death trying.

As in most Level IV prisons, there's constant racial politics. Guys are always beefing, getting stabbed. And the police are constantly getting attacked, too.

That's what gave Calipatria that reputation for being so dangerous. There was this notorious incident that happened while I was there in March 1995. A group of East Coast Crips who were lifers—dudes who felt they had nothing to lose—banded together and ran up in the program office on the A yard. They stabbed a sergeant, injured all these officers—captains, lieutenants, every officer they could find. It was like a hostile takeover. Eight cops got badly hurt.

For security reasons, the police have no handguns on the yard. The only guns are the M14s at the top of the tower. Reinforcements came rushing in from every yard in riot gear and finally got control of the situation, and Calipatria went immediately on lockdown.

And then the retribution came. Anybody on any yard who was affiliated with the East Coast Crips, even dudes who had nothing to do with the incident, all got rolled up in the middle of the night. It was two in the morning, you heard all this shouting on the tiers, and they grabbed thirty-six dudes and put them on a bus to Corcoran in nothing but their underwear. When they arrived at Corcoran, the cops were waiting with their welcome wagon. All of these dudes got the dog shit beat out of them, Rodney King style. Cops were cracking ribs, grabbing dudes by their balls, smashing their faces into the pavement. There ended up being a major investigation, and a bunch of the cops at Corcoran lost their jobs behind that shit.

So that was my new reality. That was my new day-to-day. For

those first few years in Calipatria, I just had my head down. I didn't contact nobody. Besides my mom, I didn't call my family, didn't call Ice or Trome or any of my other friends.

The first thing I needed to do was get my mind right. I had to adapt myself to the cutthroat mentality. I had to condition myself to living that Level IV lifestyle. In a place like Calipatria, it's dog-eat-dog. You get respect or you take respect. The yard is always on the verge of violence. You can't trust nobody in there.

During rec time, I became a monster on that weight pile. Channeled my focus and aggression into getting stronger. It was back to what Jamo had taught me years before at Soledad. That iron pile kept me sane. It keeps a lot of guys sane. In a place like that you can lose your mind in four or five months—never mind five years. Twenty-five years. Thirty-five years . . .

The Sureños had the largest and most unified organization, but there were strong factions of Crips and Bloods from various sets. Again, nobody gives a fuck if you were a player out in the streets. There are no distinctions between an affiliate and an active gang member. We had a couple of Harlem OGs on my yard. Any serious internal issues being made about the Harlem car, I was usually part of the decision making.

Every day, you're trying to go about your routine, productively, while in the back of your mind, you're also prepared to go to war. If it's a racial situation, if the Sureños or the whiteboys have a problem with us Blacks, you don't stop to ask questions; you've got to immediately fight alongside your race.

A racial situation might happen at eight in the morning and the Sureños' shot-caller would say: "Tonight, mandatory, everybody come to the yard. We takin' off on the Blacks." They make sure every last motherfucker that's Hispanic is on the yard with their knives on them and their boots tied. Or the Blacks can do the same thing. Every motherfucker has to fall in line, or he can expect to get DP'ed by his own people.

The main reason I wasn't in touch with anyone—for years—was because I had such a "Buck Rogers" number, I still hadn't wrapped my head around it. In the street, when you catch a long-ass sentence, we call it a "Buck Rogers" bid. It's like, "Damn, motherfucker, by the time you come home, they'll have flying cars and shit!"

We used to joke about it when I was out in the free world, but inside Calipatria—shit, there wasn't nothing funny about it.

For a long time, I just needed to be alone.

Finally, after more than three years, I decided to call one of the numbers I had for Ice's office, not sure who was going to be there.

Trome answered. "Spike!" he shouts. "Everybody wondered what happened to you!"

I brought him up to speed. "Yeah, man, I got convicted at trial. At first the DA wanted to give me the death penalty. Beat that, but we had a second trial with special circumstances—they was trying to give me LWOP. They gave me twenty-five to life plus I had to take a deal for ten more years." I remember telling him, "I don't know how the fuck I'm supposed to do thirty-five to life, Trome. You know I ain't no weak-ass motherfucker! I ain't gonna take my own life or nothin' silly like that—but how the *fuck* am I supposed to do thirty-five to life?"

I wanted to talk to Ice that day, but he wasn't around. Trome gave me a few windows to call back.

At that time, Ice was still talking to guys calling from inside. Later on, Ice changed the policy—only certain designated people would answer the phone. Mostly Al P. or Sean E. Sean or sometimes my cousin Rich would be at that number. Then they would pass your message on to Ice. Just to provide a buffer for him.

I'm calling from a wall phone at prison, and the calls go through the tower—meaning, the police listen to everything you say—so we've got to be careful. Especially talking directly to Ice, since he's the backbone of our whole organization.

Finally, I reach Ice in his recording studio, and I can hear the pain in his voice.

"Man, we heard what happened, Spike," he said. "Where you at now?"

"I'm at Calipatria State Prison, Imperial Valley, right near the Arizona border." I told him about my original sentence, plus ten more years. "Thirty-five to life. Like I was telling Trome, I don't know how I'm supposed to do this kind of time."

"Man, you should have called me," Ice says. "Maybe I could have helped. Why didn't you reach out?"

"Listen, I didn't have nobody come to the trial, I just faced that shit solo, the way a motherfucker is supposed to face it. I stayed down, man. I didn't want nobody there—my mom, my sisters, nobody. I damn sure wasn't going to call you, because I know you're out there doing your thing. Your career is going great. And you know me, man, I ain't never gonna bring no heat on you. I wasn't gonna call your phones and bring shit on you that has nothing to do with you. If the cops asked me anything about you, I said, 'I don't know no Ice-T! Go fuck yourself!'"

He didn't know the whole story of how I was facing the death penalty, but I told him. He kept saying he wanted to help, but besides sending a little money for my canteen, what could he do? There was nothing he could do. The only person who could help was *me*.

I could hear it in Ice's voice—the hurt. I was telling him the details about my case and my sentence, but what could Ice say? He was just listening. All he could do was listen.

Because, really, what *can* you say to a guy doing thirty-five to life?

ICE

Honestly, when a guy goes to prison on a life sentence, to a lot of people it's like he died. That's when you find out who's really got your back. A lot of people you thought were your homies leave you for dead. Pretty soon, they forget you even existed.

Think about it for a minute. How many people do you see on a regular basis that would notice if you simply disappeared? If you went completely off the grid? Of course, your family would be affected. But if it's a friend and someone you hang out with socially and one day you vanish, they might not even notice for a long time. And when they do—well, for a lot of people, "out of sight, out of mind." When these guys get Buck Rogers numbers, bids of twenty-five to life, thirty-five to life, LWOP, they technically *are* out of your life—because you've got to keep doing your thing. You're out there grinding, making moves, progressing, having your own ups and downs. Meanwhile, they're stuck. It's like they're frozen in time.

Hearing from Spike behind the wall after so many years, to me that was the starkest realization of the fact that we were two very similar guys who'd been on the same path, going in the same direction, and now our trajectories had split so radically.

We're not in different parts of Southern California—we're in different fucking *universes*.

Spike's calling me from that phone on the wall in a Level IV prison and I can hear it in his voice: he's strictly in survival mode. Every day inside he's making life-or-death decisions. Even the littlest shit in prison can be a mandatory fight to maintain respect. He's holding his own, no doubt, but he's stuck in the bowels of the devil.

And *my* universe? Shit, when I got that call from that penitentiary in the Imperial Valley, I was in my new house up in the Hollywood Hills. The place was huge—about ten thousand square feet, surrounded by palm trees, indoor swimming pool with retractable roof, all kinds of sculptures and paintings and aquariums. I had about ten cars, including a Lamborghini Diablo, a Range Rover, and a Rolls-Royce. I mean, as far as material things go, it was probably the peak of my high-rolling era. I was financing a real expensive lifestyle.

We'd invested a lot of money to build a state-of-the-art recording studio right in the crib—the Crackhouse we called it—and we could make our albums at home. Behind the mixing board, I had a button I could push and the whole back wall would retract to reveal this shark tank—I mean, I was playing at some James Bond villain–type shit!

But those calls from my boys in the penitentiaries were always like my reality check. They kept me grounded. It wasn't long after I talked to Spike that I went into the studio and made the song "I Must Stand," one of my most autobiographical records:

> *Streets of anger, trouble and crime*
> *I had it hard, had to sleep in my car sometimes*
> *But I never let another player see me down*
> *I kept my front up, my gear clean*
> *Even when checkin' minor green*

The musical track is down-tempo, somber. I'm breaking it all down: being orphaned at a young age, ending up in L.A., being a teen parent, going into the military, becoming a hustler and player— basically how I came from where I came from, how I ended up where I ended up at. We had an interlude that was like a snapshot of that moment in my life:

> *What?*
> *Daff is dead?*
> *Carter got twenty-five years?*
> *Spike, thirty-five to life?*
> *Nah, don't tell me B.O.'s dead, man*
> *I don't wanna hear that, man*
> *I was just with him*

We just reenacted all the bad news I was getting at that time over the phone. Michael Carter, M.C., another close player friend, had caught a long bid. B.O., one of the dudes I was close to in the Zulu Nation, had just gotten murdered in the Bronx. All this stuff was happening at the same time we found out Spike got thirty-five to life.

We know that music reaches them on the inside, so that was more than just a shout-out on a record; it was a way of sending some love to Spike, letting him know, "Yo, we're thinking about you, homie. We know you're stuck and we're here in the studio in Hollywood, but you're still on our minds."

And to the world, it was me adding yet another chapter of the cautionary tale I'm always telling in my music: These are Ice's *real* friends. These are *real* players and gangsters who used to be out in the world with Ice—balling, hustling, doing big things—and now they're either dead or in prison.

In the final verse I say:

The game is vicious, no retirement, you die young
Listen to a fake, he might tell you to grab a gun
I get phone calls from condemned row
Brothers I ran with, brothers I really know
They tell me, "Ice you got much love in the pen,
You're the one that got away, don't wanna see you in"
They tell me, "Tell the little homies the deal
Don't let 'em come up in this hellish habitat of shanks
    and steel."

SPIKE

earing the song "I Must Stand" in Calipatria was heavy—
when I got it on cassette and listened to it on the boom box
in my cell, I mean, there was a lot of mixed emotions. On the one
hand, Ice is letting me know I'm on his mind, but at the same time,
it's a reminder that I'm stuck—might never come home.

It was similar mixed feelings when Ice showed up on the TV in
my cell one night. The next day *everyone* in Calipatria was talking
about him. Everything in a Level IV is so structured and controlled,
little things like your TV programs become super important. You'll
plan out a whole week based on what you're trying to watch. Some
dudes watch the evening news religiously. Or the Lakers games.

We had a thirteen-inch TV in our cell, and every Thursday night,
I would watch *New York Undercover*. Because it was an urban drama
with young Black and Hispanic stars, because they featured so much
hip-hop, that was one of the shows that people in prison watched
every week. And out of the clear blue, one Thursday evening, I see
Ice as a guest star!

What the fuck?

I just freeze, glued to the TV, wondering where this plotline is
going. Ice is playing this chemist drug kingpin Danny Cort. They call
him "Danny Up."

Ice really *became* that character; he transformed into that crazy
chemist. Aggressive. Vindictive. Psychopathic. Sinister as fuck. He's
the archnemesis to Malik Yoba's character J. C. Williams. There's this

moment when Danny Up shows up unexpectedly at the door with a bunch of roses for J. C.'s pregnant fiancée, Sandy, and I'm saying, "Look at my boy fixin' to take this broad out!" And that's what he did. Danny killed her with a machine gun, right before the wedding day—shit, it blew my mind.

That became a defining moment in Calipatria. Damn near everybody in the prison was watching that episode, and the next day, it's all you heard dudes talking about on the yard.

"You see *New York Undercover* last night? That nigga Ice was wild."

"Ice was with the business, man."

I'm listening to people saying all this shit, but I'm hesitant to join in. I can't say what's really in my head. I can't tell any of these guys, "Yeah, that's my boy. Dude's like a brother to me."

I can't tell them that long before the fame, this is a player who I ran with, this is a guy I hit licks with, this is a brother who slept on my mom's couch.

When you're in a Level IV prison, nobody wants to hear all that shit. First off, motherfuckers think you're lying. "Oh, you know Ice-T? Then what the fuck are you doing here? How'd you end up catching a life sentence? What happened?"

They think because you've got a successful friend, he can somehow undo the mistakes you've made on your *own*.

Also, the mentality of the dudes in a Level IV is different from other prisons. In a Level I or Level II, you might be around guys doing eighteen months or three years, so they've still got their mind on the streets, on coming home soon. But in a Level IV, the average motherfucker is doing some serious time. Fifteen or twenty years at a minimum. And you got motherfuckers with Buck Rogers numbers. Fifty years. One hundred years. Two hundred years. LWOP. They've already accepted that prison is their reality. Forever. They know they ain't never leaving alive. When they get out, it'll be feetfirst, in a body bag on a gurney.

These dudes don't give a fuck about who you used to run with. They don't give a fuck about who you know that's famous. They don't want to hear your war stories from the streets. They just want to be left alone, trying to do their time productively, hitting that iron pile. Living whatever little piece of life they've got left. They're trying to make it through their prison existence, moment by fucking moment.

Whenever I hear Ice's name mentioned, I'm telling myself, *That's my crew, that's my family, that's part of who I am.*

But I kept all my thoughts to myself.

Every new step that Ice took in his career, I was proud of him. Extremely proud. From hip-hop to heavy metal, starring in movies and on TV, he was constantly breaking barriers—I could see how his life was just steadily heading upward.

I'm looking at it all through the lens of a thirteen-inch television in my hot-as-hell prison cell. And I'm also feeling demoralized. I'm feeling down. Because I know I should have been out there for all of this. When the whole yard was talking about how dope Ice was on *New York Undercover,* I just kept telling myself:

Man, you fucked up!

I had been part of something special. I was going places, before I caught this life sentence. In Calipatria, it felt like I was banished to the desert, exiled from the kingdom.

ICE

When I did that role of Danny Cort on *New York Undercover*, it really hit home with a lot of the brothers who were locked up. That particular show lit up the penitentiaries. On the inside, television gets played over and over. Dudes can't necessarily watch new movies—don't see the stuff that comes out in the theaters—but a popular TV show definitely penetrates the walls.

I wasn't even planning on getting into TV. By 1995, I had a few solid movies under my belt: *Trespass*, *Ricochet*, and *Surviving the Game*. But taking on the role of Danny Cort really changed the whole rest of my career, because it was my first time working for Dick Wolf. It led to me landing a role on *Law & Order* and relocating my whole life to New York.

One of my mottoes is "You don't guide life; you ride life." Again, me transitioning to TV just happened kind of randomly, because I was sitting around talking shit.

I was at my house with my friend Fab 5 Freddy. We were by my pool chopping it up. Freddy was in one of his artistic zones, having some wild creative idea about how I should build a planetarium in my house, and he got a phone call from Andre Harrell—rest in peace. Freddy said, "Yo, I'm sitting here with Ice-T."

"Hey, tell Ice to come on *New York Undercover*."

Andre was one of the producers of the show. I'd known him for years, since he was rapping in the duo Dr. Jeckyll & Mr. Hyde.

I started teasing him. "Fuck your show, man! It's just a rip-off of *New Jack City*."

"Oh, you're too *big* to help a brother now that you're living in the Hollywood Hills?"

"Dig, give me a bad-guy role and I'll come on."

Actors want to go from one extreme to the other. I'd done my thing as an undercover cop in *New Jack City*. Now I wanted to be some evil-as-fuck villain.

"Okay, if we get you a bad-guy part, you'll do it?"

"Yeah, give me a fucking sinister motherfucker and I'm in."

They had to switch up the part for me, because the role of Danny Cort was written for a white actor. He was supposed to be a brilliant chemist who was cooking up meth—this was in the days before most people even knew what meth was.

They got me the script, and the producers let me go crazy with it. I mean, I was a true psychopath. I shot Malik Yoba's pregnant fiancée with a machine gun. Held his son hostage and played Russian roulette with him. I had a blast taking it to the extreme. I was an archcriminal.

And after I did the first episode, Dick Wolf said, "Ice, I don't want to kill your character, will you stay on? We want you to do two more episodes." I wasn't making any money for the role—it was costing me my entire check just to stay in a hotel in Manhattan with Sean E. Sean being my assistant. So they bumped up my accommodations to the Four Seasons, took care of Sean's expenses, and we shot two more. That was the beginning of my history with Dick Wolf.

We heard from a lot of the brothers in prison about Danny Cort—not only from Spike. *New York Undercover* was really big on the inside. The media and critical response was positive, too. The NAACP gave me an Image Award for Best Supporting Actor in a TV drama.

But of course it had to be mixed feelings for Spike, watching all this good shit happening for me, knowing he should have been there for the whole ride. He should have been hanging out with us at my pool in the Hollywood Hills, going to award shows, traveling the world. Before he got locked up, he was supposed to come with us on the first Body Count tour of Europe in 1993.

And if he'd been free, he *would* have been there. That's the truth. He would have been part of all of it.

SPIKE

During those first years I was in Calipatria, besides feeling like I fucked up with Ice, one of the main things I was dealing with was the damage my actions were causing within my family. There was a whole lot of guilt, man. A whole lot of guilt.

Before I fell, I had this ugly situation with my oldest brother, Terry. He was so much older than me—seven years—when I was a little kid, I used to look up to him as an OG. He was "Turk," one of the founding generation of the Harlem Godfathers. He got me my first car. Terry was always in the streets, but he never made real money—he was a pimp, a small-time PCP dealer. Hustling-wise, it was minor-league stuff. He was really more about the gangbanging life.

In my era, I started making major money. And there was always kind of a jealousy factor—Terry felt left out. Even though I took him on a few licks, there was always a feeling like he was being left behind, always some kind of tension between us.

And right before I fell, Terry stole from me. I had a bag with $250,000 worth of loose diamonds hidden at my sister's house. Those diamonds were already sold; I had a fence downtown ready to give me $80,000 cash. Clint and me hit that lick together, so half of that score belonged to him.

Terry broke into my sister's house, found the bag, and stole it—went to the local dope dealer and sold a quarter-million worth of diamonds for a measly *ounce* of cocaine.

When I found out, I was so angry, I went over to my sister's looking for him. "Where is that motherfucker? When I catch him, I'm gonna kill him."

My mother heard me saying all this, and it shocked her. When we left, Clint said, "You shouldn't have said all that to your mom. You need to go back and apologize." He was right; that was the first time I ever cursed or talked like a street dude in front of her. Even though I lost all those diamonds, I still owed Clint his forty G's, so that had to come out of my own pocket. I went back and apologized to my mother, but I was still furious. "Forgive me, Mom. I'm not going to take his life, but if I catch him, I *am* going to hurt him."

Then I fell and nothing was resolved between us. I still had all this anger. When I first got to Calipatria, I called my mom's house and my brother accepted the collect call.

"Who's this?"

"It's Terry."

Hearing his voice was such a shock, I just unloaded with both barrels. "What the fuck are you doing on my mother's phone? If I would've caught you, I would've killed your motherfucking ass. You sold all those diamonds for some bullshit!"

"I apologize, man, I was getting high. I'm going to pay you back."

"Fuck you! You ain't my brother no more. You ain't shit. Put my mother on the phone."

At that moment, at that phase of my life, I didn't have enough maturity to forgive my brother. I didn't have the maturity to under-stand the battles he was fighting with addiction. I knew he was smok-ing crack. I knew he was hooked on that shit. In that state of being fucked up, high, and needing money, he stole from me.

Thinking about it now, the craziest thing is this: I was furious with my brother for stealing from me, when I was stealing from *everybody*.

I was reading him the riot act for taking $250,000 worth of dia-monds from me—when it was stolen merchandise in the first place!

When Terry answered the phone unexpectedly, I was so angry, I hung up on my mother. When I called back a few days later, she said, "Baby, I'm trying to tell you something. Your brother's not using drugs no more. He's clean. He's been coming to church with me for a long while."

I had a chance to make amends with Terry, but I didn't. Instead, I cursed him out and said he was dead to me. To this day, that phone call haunts me, because those were the last words I ever spoke to my brother.

But the greatest guilt I felt was about my daughter, Marquise. When I first fell, my daughter cried for weeks. She was only seven years old. She wouldn't come out of her bedroom. Even though I was a full-time player and a hustler, when she was little, I tried to be there for her. She didn't know I was living this double life in the streets. When I came back to the house in Bakersfield, I turned my pagers off, I wasn't on the phone with my homies.

When my daughter was small, I made a point of spending a lot of quality time with her. Taking her skating, taking her to see Hulk Hogan wrestle. We spent Sundays at the beach or at Magic Mountain. During the week, I'd sit there helping her with homework.

And she took so much after me. Everyone would say she was the spitting image of me. And since she was my only child, everyone always asked about her. "How's Marquise, Spike?" They knew that little girl was my heart.

But when I was taken into custody in October 1992, things started to deteriorate between her mom and me. Before the trial, when I was in the San Diego County Jail, she did drive out there to see me a couple of times and brought my daughter. I remember sitting there behind the glass talking to my daughter for fifteen minutes on the phone as her mother held the receiver to her ear. And she was putting her little hands on the glass, and I put my hands against her hands on the glass, palm to palm, trying to touch her.

I would just stare into her eyes and get closer to the glass until we were eyeball to eyeball. When you're on a no-contact jail visit like that, you can look in your daughter's eyes and see how much she loves you but there's also a confused expression, like, "Daddy, why aren't you coming home? I miss you!"

I can remember the way she'd cry when the visits would end. Broke my heart. I'd get cuffed, and as the police led me back to my cell, I'd be talking to myself. "Man, I don't want to keep putting her through all this shit."

After a while her mother stopped even coming to the county jail. You see, it all came out at trial that I was a player—had different broads—and they came to court to testify for the prosecution about my character. They all said I was this flashy motherfucker who always carried a lot of cash and drove fancy cars and all that shit. Each one of these broads testified that she thought she was my girlfriend. My daughter's mom was the only one who didn't come to court to testify.

From the moment the detectives said they were going to make an example of my ass, boy, they meant that shit! They had me under surveillance for all those months I was doing what I was doing, and that task force was taking pictures of everything. They had me coming in and out of the homes of different broads, or them riding in my Mercedes, my Corvette, and my Trans Am. When I was locked up, they showed all the photos to my daughter's mom.

"Look, he's fucking with this girl and he's fucking with that girl."

These cops were doing everything in the book to get her to co-operate. And she never would, but it poisoned her to the point that she wouldn't visit me or even accept my phone calls.

I would write her letters and say, "Please come bring my daughter—I want to see her." But she wouldn't. I said, "At least let her hear my voice on the phone, I want to tell her I love her." But I couldn't even talk to my daughter. Her mom wouldn't accept the calls.

And then, as I started to serve my prison sentence at Calipatria, my daughter decided that she didn't want any kind of relationship with me.

I had to accept that.

I'd write letters that she wouldn't answer.

When you catch a life sentence, there's this ripple effect.

When I was doing time, my daughter was doing time. Why? Because like a lot of dads to their little girls, I was like her Superman. And when that bond between us was broken, it was the worst thing that can happen between a father and child.

At first, I was rationalizing it. I felt like other people were to blame—the cops and her mom were removing her from my life. But now I'd flip it around and put it this way: *my* bad decisions removed me from her life.

Despite all the mistakes I made, yes, I loved her so much. I still do.

We're continuing to deal with the damage. She's in her thirties and still feels that I let her down. I remember her saying to me, "Dad, how come you couldn't stop doing this?"

That haunts me, too. Because there's no answer. Nothing I can ever say will fix the years of hurt. As a father, that hits you like a body blow, hearing those words from your daughter:

"Dad, didn't you love me enough to stop doing all the wrong you were doing?"

CHAPTER 10

THE WEIGHT

Sentenced to prison
Had niggas up against real shit
Recipe to turn niggas into monsters
Beneath them towers
Prison politics carried out
You ain't gon' follow, get you DP'd, stomped out
PC'd, dogged out, busted on, found out
Paperwork faulty
Them savage niggas'll run up in your house
                    —*SPIKE, "OUTSIDE LOOKING IN"*

SPIKE

Then in the spring of 1996, the deaths started. One after another, all these people in my life began to die. When you're in prison on a life sentence and you get news of a death on the outside, that's when reality comes into sharp focus really fast.

Someone you love is gone, they're having the funeral, and you're not there; you're stuck in this fucking dungeon in the desert—I mean, the consequences of your bad choices get amplified a thousand times.

Besides Ice, of all the guys in Body Count, I was closest to Vic. Beatmaster V was never a jewel thief, we never hit any licks together—but to me, he was always one of the flyest, most loyal motherfuckers. Vic was a true player. I remember sitting around his house on Slauson and Tenth Avenue, watching him at his drum kit, playing along to Led Zeppelin records for fun.

I was at the wall phone in Calipatria for my fifteen-minute call and when I dialed Ice's office, Cousin Rich answered. We chopped it up for a minute, then he says, "Yo, Spike, somebody wants to talk to you."

Beatmaster V grabbed the phone. I hadn't talked to Vic in over four years.

"Spike, listen, Body Count's a hit, baby! We gonna help you out, man. I'm gonna send you forty or fifty thousand like it ain't shit. But listen, when you get home, stay out of trouble!"

I laughed. "Man, listen, if I ever get home, Vic, I'm square as a pool table, twice as green."

Vic didn't know all the details of my case; he didn't know money wasn't going to help get me out of a life sentence for murder. Realistically, the only use I would have for money was if—and that was a *big* if—I ever had a date in front of the board. Then I could retain a private attorney who specialized in parole hearings and not just rely on a public defender.

But what Vic said wasn't really about money.

Just by offering to help, he was sending some love.

Before he got off the phone, he said, "Hey, I wanna send you some pictures—give me your address, player."

I gave him my CDC number and the P.O. box at Calipatria, and about a week later, I got a letter with snapshots from Vic. He was standing in front of his crib on Slauson. He'd just bought a brand-new two-door Benz and an Alfa Romeo. He had on his jewelry and was standing there with his arms in the air with this look on his face that said, "Spike, we made it, baby!"

I felt so proud of Vic and all the guys, and I called back at Ice's office number two weeks later to thank him for the pictures. This time it was Al P. who answered.

"Vic's gone, Spike."

"When's he gonna be back?"

"Vic's *gone*. He died."

"Fuck you talking about, Trome?"

"Vic passed in his sleep."

"Stop bullshitting, man."

"For real, Spike, Vic died of cancer."

"What? I just talked to him! I just got the pictures he sent me in the mail."

Trome explained that Vic had been sick for a while, battling leukemia, but the band hadn't been telling anyone.

Standing there at the wall phone in the day room, I felt all the wind knocked out of me.

I got a chance to talk to Vic that one time and hear him so happy, on top of the world, and now he's fucking dead?

The pictures had given me a bit of hope. Imagining us all hanging out together one day again, I visualized Vic practicing his drums to Led Zeppelin in his crib, all of us laughing, back together like old times.

I hung up that wall phone and walked back to my cell, still not really believing it, trying to wrap my head around the fact that I'd never see my homie Vic again.

ICE

When Vic died, it shook everybody up. Spike was dealing with it on the inside, and we were dealing with it on the outside.

Nobody saw it coming. Vic was in great shape. He looked like an athlete—he wasn't bodybuilder big, but he was muscular and really took care of himself. In 1995, we first got the word that Vic had leukemia. We were all such young dudes, to be honest, I wasn't even sure what leukemia was, but they explained it was cancer of the blood, and he was going to need a bone-marrow transplant from his brother.

We were on tour in Belgium in the summer '95. We had a sold-out concert and Vic was looking really weak. Ever since his diagnosis, Vic would constantly get blood tests. The doctor said with the blood count he had, he was technically dead. I canceled the concert. People gave us shit for that, but I was like, "I'm not going to have my friend dying onstage!" We never told anyone he had cancer. We just said he was sick. Vic didn't want anyone outside our circle to know how serious a situation it was.

Eight months later, in April '96, he was dead.

It broke my heart, just like it broke Spike's heart. It was such a fucked-up situation. When one of your childhood friends dies and he's only in his thirties, you really can't make sense of it. I don't go to funerals as a rule. I'd much rather remember the person alive. I don't want to see someone I love lying there in a box. But I made it a point to go to Vic's. I sat there at his funeral crying and, I mean, people who know me had *never* seen me cry.

The timing of it was so cold. This was just the moment when all the guys in Body Count were starting to make some money, enjoying the fruits of success. We'd left Warner Bros. after the "Cop Killer" controversy, and I had gone to our new label, Virgin Records, and asked for a million dollars cash up front for our next record.

Ernie and Vic are driving around in brand-new cars, everybody's looking like a rock star. We're recording our third album, *Violent Demise*, and suddenly Vic is dead.

Then the next year, we lost Mooseman. Moose went back to his old neighborhood—Rollin' 60s—and was standing in a driveway talking with some of his friends and a car drove up and starting shooting, hit Moose in his back, and killed him on the spot. He was the only person who really didn't have to be there. Moose was never a gangbanger, didn't even live in the neighborhood anymore. He was just coming back to see his old friends.

Then D-Roc—the Executioner—our rhythm guitarist, passed from cancer. He'd been fighting lymphoma for a long time. So it's one blow after the next, three of our band members gone.

Three young dudes—all unexpected, all in a short period of time.

Of the original members of Body Count, it was down to me and Ernie C. It felt like every time we'd try to get the group back together to make a new record or plan a tour, somebody else would die, and we'd be in a state of mourning. It was a dark period.

I remember saying, "The name Body Count is starting to sound too fucking prophetic, you know?"

SPIKE

Two weeks later I called to hear about Vic's funeral and Trome answers at the office. He brought me up to speed, then he said, "Hey, Spike, Bruce is trying to reach out to you."

"Really?"

"He's trying to send you some money, homie. You got a pencil?"

By this time, Bruce Richardson was one of the richest players in L.A. And I knew how generous he could be. He was already a millionaire in the early 1980s, but now—by 1995—he had some *serious* paper. He owned a club at the bottom of the Beverly Center called the World. All the ballers and players from the hood used to hang out there.

Trome told me the place you could always catch Bruce or leave a message was at Genius Car Wash on Crenshaw. He gave me the number, I jotted it down, and my next phone slot, I tried to call Bruce. No answer. I kept trying, and the phone just kept ringing at Genius Car Wash.

Finally, a week later, I called back to Ice's office and Trome says, "I got bad news for you, man. They got your boy."

"What?"

"They got Bruce. He's dead."

"You're bullshitting me, man."

He starts telling me that Bruce got murdered, but I'm on that wall phone and the police in the tower are monitoring everything. I said, "Nah, nah, nah." Meaning, don't get into any specifics on this phone.

News from the street reached inside real fast; I found out the details on the yard. Bruce was shot and killed inside his house under really suspicious circumstances.

Bruce was a tall, powerful dude and he was a martial artist— and the day before he got killed he'd smacked the shit out of this one notorious gangster and his bodyguards in his club. Whether there was any connection to his murder, nobody could say for sure. To this day, there's a lot of weird rumors and mystery surrounding his death.

In the space of a couple weeks in '96, two of my partners, two of the most loyal dudes, Vic and Bruce, are both suddenly gone.

Karma will do that to you, man—give you a little sliver of hope and then slam the door in your motherfucking face.

✻   ✻   ✻

It wasn't long before death started to hit even closer to home.

One afternoon, the mail comes around, and I see a letter from my grandmother. She was writing to me from the hospital, on her deathbed.

Alton, trust in God for all things in your life and read the word of God each day and say a Sinner's Prayer. Talk to God, and He will hear you.

God loves people but He wants us to give ourselves to Him and we'll know how to live for him by helping others come to Him.

Alton, turn from the life of sin and repeat a Sinner's Prayer. He will give you a new heart to serve Him and help others come to Him. Say a Sinner's Prayer and be washed in the blood of Jesus Christ our Savior.

It was a three-page letter, and as I was reading the last page, I felt my heart race. My grandmother stopped addressing me and wrote directly to God on my behalf.

Heavenly Father, I dedicate my grandson Alton unto You that he would be raised as You desire and follow the path that You would choose.

Heavenly Father, I commit myself as a grandparent to train my grandson in the way he should go, trusting in the promise that he will not depart from Your ways, but grow and prosper in them.

I turn the care and burden of raising him unto thee, Dear
God. I will do as the word of God commands from the Bible.

I'm sitting there on my bunk, reading that letter over and over, and my heart kept racing faster.

It felt like I was in an elevator, dropping down the shaft without any cord holding me up.

I was free-falling into the void, talking to myself in my cell.

"Do you understand the cold choices you made and how they affected your grandmother and your mother? Do you understand the cold decisions you've been making throughout your whole mother-fucking life? You not only paid the price with your freedom, Spike, you paid the price by letting people down, having people you love die and you not being out in the world to help."

Writing that letter to me was one of the last things my grandmother did. That's what really froze me, realizing that from the hospital, when *she* was dying, my grandmother took the time to write me a letter urging me to change my sinner's heart and asking God to intercede on my behalf.

Heavenly Father, I dedicate my grandson Alton unto You that he
would be raised as You desire and follow the path that You would choose.

I immediately said the Sinner's Prayer, just as she'd asked me to. I knew exactly what passage of Scripture she meant for me to read.

John 9:31 from the King James Bible.

Now we know that God heareth not sinners: but if any man
be a worshipper of God, and doeth his will, him he heareth.

✧   ✧   ✧

That letter from my grandmother sparked a desire to do something more than just *survive* in a Level IV. One way or another, I wanted to get transferred to a prison closer to my family. A couple years into my bid at Calipatria, I managed to get a job as an office clerk. That was an important step if I was going to lower my points to be classified in a Level III or Level II. It was tough to get an office job in a maximum-security prison like Calipatria. The only reason I got it was because I won this weightlifting contest on C yard.

I wasn't the strongest guy on that yard—not by a fucking long shot. But I set my mind on winning the contest and figured out how I could do it. There were three lifts for combined points: bench press, dead lift, and squat. Most of these guys were a lot stronger than me on the bench. These big ol' swole individuals—two-hundred-eighty-pound, three-hundred-pound guys—that been down forever and could bench way over five hundred. But when I looked at them, I realized some of these huge dudes had carrot legs. On the squat rack, even with relatively light weights, their legs would be shaking like minibikes.

Every day we went out to that iron pile, I strategized like we would in the finesse game. *Don't go against their strengths, you'll never be able to bench what these guys can. Just concentrate on your lower body—dead lifts and squats.*

I'd been doing squats seriously for a few years, but now I started to increase the weights. I got hooked on the challenge of it, mastering the art of squatting and deadlifting. Because your legs and back are some of the strongest muscles you've got—after your heart. It's mostly a question of mentality. Especially in prison, where you can't really eat a good diet. You've got to get your mind right. I found that I was strongest on a nearly empty stomach; I'd just eat half a banana and a drink a cup of coffee in the morning.

The contest consisted of three powerlifts for combined points: first bench press, then dead lift, and finally squats. This worked out perfectly for me: I had my strategy worked out in advance. Since my bench wasn't near what these bigger guys could do, I'd have to take them out by targeting their weakness—those damn carrot legs.

The day of the contest, guys started dropping by the wayside, and it came down to me and this big ol' country dude who was about two-seventy, outweighing me by more than forty pounds. Like I expected, he blew me away on the bench press. On the dead lift, I put up over five hundred pounds, making sure I had just enough points for the final lift—my strongest—the squat.

When he went to the squat rack, he got up under ten quarters—five hundred pounds—and I saw he was struggling to hit that shit. I did my squat for five hundred without any trouble. On his next lift, this guy tried to put a dime on each side. The bar airplaned before the spotters could catch it, and a fifty-pound plate flew off and broke my friend's foot.

They took my friend to the clinic. And now the homies are really egging me on:

"Spike, shut this motherfucker down."

"Look," I said, "put fifty more motherfucking pounds on each side."

"What the fuck?"

"You heard me, put a hundred more pounds on this shit."

I wasn't bullshitting around—I was going straight to six hundred pounds. I was fixing to end the contest with one lift.

I get up under that weight, let it settle on my traps, take it off that rack. Everyone gets quiet. I take two steps forward, lock my jaw, grit my teeth. Then I sat down with all that weight and got up nice and steady.

"Oh shit!"

With that one lift, I jumped fifty points clear, and wasn't nobody catching me.

Throughout the contest, this white lieutenant named Patterson had been watching, and he said he wanted to talk. He was an older dude, silvery hair, near retirement age, but he'd once been a power-lifter. He was impressed at my technique and the fact that at 228 pounds, I could squat six hundred. I walked over to him and he asked my name.

"Alton Pierce."

"Pierce, how long you been squatting heavy like that?"

"About three years."

"Only three years? Shit, that's impressive."

We talked a bit about training and technique; he took an interest in helping me out.

"Where do you work, Pierce?"

"These people won't give me no damn job, sir. They're giving me the runaround. I been waiting like fifteen fucking months, but nobody's got an answer for me in the inmate assignment office."

This lieutenant had a lot of juice and said he'd get me a job as a clerk in the watch office, where he'd heard a vacancy was opening up.

"Do you know how to type?"

"Honestly, no. I'm not very good at typing, sir."

"Don't worry about it. You can learn how to type. You can start off as a porter, and the other clerks will show you the ropes."

It took a while to come through, but I landed the clerk's job in the watch office, outside the main B yard. Throughout the day, the watch office was filled with the top brass, some civilians. The job paid seventy cents per hour—believe it or not, that's considered a good rate on the inside—and was a highly desirable placement as far as prison work goes. I was one of only three clerks and the only Black dude working there.

There was this chaplain, an older Irish priest, named Father Dermody, who used to come around from time to time. About six-one, always in his priest's collar and black suit, a real kindly older guy. But I started to dread seeing his face because whenever he came to see me, he was the bearer of bad news. The first time, I was sitting there at the typewriter, and I hear this soft voice with a strong Irish accent.

"Alton Pierce?" Father Dermody says, walking into the watch office. "I need you to follow me back to the yard. You can have a phone call, son."

"What's this about?"

"I'm sorry, son. You've had a death in the family."

My heart was racing the whole walk through the yard. I called home and learned that my brother Terry was dead. All I could think about were those last words to him.

Fuck you! You ain't my brother no more! You ain't shit. Put my mother on the phone!

Our *last* conversation—and I had been filled with so much rage. He was trying to apologize to me, but all I could think about was those stolen diamonds and I kept telling him to go fuck himself.

It took a while before I learned all the details. My brother was murdered in a rival neighborhood. The cops found him tied up in a van, strangled. He was going to see a female and he crossed neighborhood lines, and when the bangers over there found out he was from the 30s, that he was Big Turk, an original Harlem Godfather, they snatched him up and killed him. When you go to the wrong areas in L.A. and you're really about that gangbanging life like Turk was, it can quickly turn fatal.

When I found out my brother was dead, I fell to my knees in my cell and asked God for forgiveness that I didn't make amends with him on that phone call.

This dark cloud of death kept hanging over me in Calipatria. Only two weeks after my brother died, I find out that my father is in the hospital with lung cancer. No one in my family wanted to tell me about it. My niece who I hadn't talked to in years wrote me a letter to tell me that my dad had cancer and he needed a lung transplant. She said he was already skinny as a toothpick. When the mail arrived, I just sat there with tears rolling down my cheeks.

He loved all of us, but he wasn't around a lot when I was growing up. Between all his time in the service, his two tours of Vietnam, he never really got a chance to see me play baseball, even when I was a star on the high school team. I think he made it to one game.

When I learned he had cancer I was thinking about the times my dad would take me fishing in Malibu or at Seal Beach. We'd leave the house at 2 a.m.; I was just seven years old, sleepwalking to the car with the tackle box and rods. We'd always stop to get Doritos and 7-Up on the way. Even today, when I see a bag of Doritos it makes me think of going fishing with my dad.

We'd had our differences over the years, but I loved my dad a lot and wanted to see him again.

When I got him on the phone, he sounded weak, but he was downplaying how sick he really was.

"Man, don't worry about me," he said. "I know you're going to get out of there."

"Dad, I don't know if I'm ever coming home. You can have one of my lungs. If I'm gonna die in prison, I'd rather something of mine be free."

I talked to him about a week later and it was obvious he was saying goodbye. They were telling him he had months to live, but the cancer was so advanced, he could go at any time.

"I love you," he said. "All I want you to do is come home and be with your daughter."

"Stop talking like that, Dad," I said. "I'm gonna work on getting a hardship transfer, so I can be at a prison closer to L.A. We'll see each other—just stop talking like you're leaving us."

After getting that letter from my grandmother asking God to intercede and change my heart, I decided I'd start to go to this little church at Calipatria. They used to have coffee and donuts on Sunday, and I would sit there and pray silently. I started to ask some hard questions of myself.

All this death, all this pain—was there a higher purpose behind it? Was it God's way of making me feel the destruction I'd caused within someone else's family?

Because of the crime that I committed, because of the cold choices that I made, someone wasn't going to be at the dinner table tonight with his loved ones. Even though I wasn't the person who pulled the trigger, I was just as culpable—I was *more* culpable, in fact, because I put the whole robbery together. None of it would have happened without my selfishness and scheming.

Sitting in that little chapel, I realized each one of these deaths was like a new weight I had to carry. Another hundred pounds on my shoulders. And this wasn't a contest on the iron pile where I could just drop that fucking six hundred pounds back on the rack.

This burden wasn't going anywhere.

I was going to carry this weight around, without rest, for the remainder of my life.

CHAPTER 11

MY MOTHER'S SON

Pockets near empty
The borderline of being broke
Dreamin' they blowin' my brains out
So stayin' woke
Hear the Lord calling me home
Similar to Mom's strictest curfews
When streetlights comin' on
      —SPIKE, "FORTY DAYS AND FORTY NIGHTS"

SPIKE

The whole time I was in Calipatria I didn't have any visits from family or friends; no one was driving all that way from L.A. into that hot-ass desert in the Imperial Valley. Ice and me came up with the idea of doing a charity concert. Calipatria didn't have a proper library and there was a music room without any instruments, so I was thinking we could raise money to help the prison make some improvements and give the inmates some educational incentives.

Also, I was looking forward to seeing everybody I hadn't seen in years. I gave them a list of people who were coming with Ice, and they ran a security check on everybody's name: Cousin Rich, Sean E. Sean, Al P., Sean E. Mac, Evil E. The problem was, most of them got denied because they'd done time before.

There's so much red tape involved in planning a concert in prison, it took us almost two months to get signatures. Finally, we locked in a date. Ice was scheduled to come perform at Calipatria on June 11, 1998.

The only signature we were waiting on to move forward was the warden, and he was on vacation. This captain named Emma Rodriguez was the acting warden. I knew her personally and we always got along fine. I used to see her every day in the watch office where I was a clerk. She calls a meeting in the programs office. I'm the only inmate in the room, just a bunch of captains, lieutenants, and sergeants. But Captain Rodriguez is talking to us through an intercom in another building.

I thought the meeting was just to finalize the logistics of the event, but her first question completely threw me:

"Didn't Ice-T make 'Cop Killer'?"

I'm thinking somebody must have got in her ear, because instead of signing off on the concert, she launches into this full-blown interrogation, hitting me with all these questions about whether Ice was going to incite violence against the police or start a race riot.

"Ice-T's not going to cause any problems here, ma'am," I said.

"Is Ice-T a Crip or a Blood?" she asked.

"He isn't a gang member, ma'am," I said. "He's an entertainer, a musician. He performs all over the world. He's performed inside San Quentin. He's no threat, ma'am. He's no different than me. You've been around me in the watch office. Did I appear to be a threat to you?"

The more of these pointed questions she asked, the more I started to think about the potential downside to Ice in terms of bad publicity. He was basically doing a free concert as a favor to me, and it could result in all kinds of negative blowback for him. The last thing Ice needed was for another flare-up of the "Cop Killer" controversy.

"Ma'am, look, my friend doesn't deserve all this. All we were trying to do is put on a charity event and raise money for something positive. He's willing to take time out of his schedule to drive all the way from Los Angeles to the Imperial Valley, but if you've got concerns about security and him being a risk, we can just call this off."

One of the captains in the room said, "Pierce, hold on, we'll work this out." Because it was a huge thing that Ice was going to come, and even a bunch of the staff were looking forward to it.

"No, we're good, we're good. I'll let Ice know that it's off."

During my next phone slot, I called Ice at his office and explained.

"Look, man, they trippin'. I apologize."

A week later, the real warden was back—he pulled me out of the line at breakfast, wanting to know exactly what happened.

"When you were on vacation, sir, the acting warden had all kinds of security concerns, so we shut it down."

The warden gave me this look like he was genuinely disappointed. "Why don't you have Ice-T call me and we can talk about it?" he said.

I didn't even relay the message to Ice. I didn't want to start the whole process again, only to have them pull the rug out from under us over some bullshit.

ICE

Performing for cats on the inside is different. I did one show with Paul Rodriguez at San Quentin and that was deep. Whenever we get the call to come to one of these prisons, I say, "Cool," but then there's a long-ass screening process and you just never know how it's going to play out. Every prison is different. You can't have any felonies on your record. Nearly everyone in my crew—Sean E. Sean, Al P., Sean E. Mac, Big Rich—all of them have done time and can't get the clearance to come with me.

When Spike put together the idea of me coming to Calipatria to do a charity event, we were waiting for the green light, but honestly, I don't think it was ever going to happen. Spike was at a Level IV. A super-violent joint. That place was just too high-powered. Somebody in the administration was always going to find an excuse to squash it at the last minute.

Our friend Michael Carter *did* manage to get us into the place where he was doing time, High Desert State Prison. But Michael Carter was such a fucking player, man! He finessed it, ran some slick game, playing one warden against the other. Spike tried to do everything by the book; Mike did the opposite. He waited till the real warden was out of town and somehow persuaded the acting warden that the show was all preapproved, and the next thing we know we get a call saying, "It's a go." Al P., Sean E. Sean, Rich— everybody with felony convictions, they still came inside with me. We literally walked into that prison with anvil cases. Nobody even checked our equipment. We could have had machine guns in those motherfuckers!

They escort us inside, and there's Michael Carter wearing Gucci glasses and gators—in *prison*. He was dressed like a club promoter, had a greenroom set up with catering and everything. We did a full performance in the gym. I did "Original Gangster," "Colors," "6 'N the Mornin'," "New Jack Hustler"—all my hard-core shit, didn't tone anything down. It was like any other concert on the outside; the only way you knew you were in a prison is because when it came time to leave, nobody could come out with us. Other than that, you know, the inmates were in charge, and we all had a great fucking time.

Once we left, that's when Mike caught some static. He went in the hole for two months after the warden came back and got pissed off—because the show hadn't been approved at all!

But Mike said that two months in the hole was worth it because of the juice he got off of that one show. He rode his bid out from that juice. He came out of the hole and the whole prison treated him like a king.

That's the mind of a player. I remember Mike laughing about it later:

"Sometimes it's better to ask for forgiveness than permission."

SPIKE

After that charity show fell through, I did get some positive news. I found out that my hardship transfer request was approved, and I was scheduled to be moved to Lancaster, just twenty-five minutes north of L.A., where at least maybe I could have some face-to-face contact with family members.

All my property was packed up and waiting to be shipped, and then some craziness jumped off on January 3, 1999.

The Sureños and the Blacks got into a major race riot. All of Calipatria ended up in a state of emergency that lasted more than six months.

It all started when this Eight Tray Gangster named Insane Mike was trying to light a cigarette in his cell by putting two prongs of a paper clip into an electrical socket. He wound up blowing the whole power grid on the wall on that tier. His next-door neighbor was the shot-caller of the Sureños. It was a weekend, so that meant no power—no TV programs—and the shot-caller was really pissed off.

The Sureños called a meeting with the guy who had the keys to car for the Eight Trays, a lifer named Mac-10, and immediately they demanded that the ETGs roll Insane Mike off the yard. Mac-10 tells them straight up, "Listen, don't no other fucking race dictate shit to us. We'll handle this how we see fit to handle it."

Just like what happened when I was at Susanville, when you start shot-calling to another race, you're crossing the motherfucking line.

Mac-10 hits the yard to talk to all the different Crip sets. This shit affects all Crips, even Rollin' 60s, who are longtime enemies of Eight Trays. None of the internal Crip politics matters if something kicks off between the Hispanics and the Blacks. Most of us were still in the blind—it wasn't our building where the incident happened—and when we heard that the Sureños' shot-caller told the ETGs to roll Insane Mike off the yard, every single one of us was outraged.

"Fuck no," I said. "He ain't snitched on nobody. He ain't no child molester. What the fuck are you going roll him up for? Because he blew out a light socket?"

Maybe the ETGs could DP him by sending three homies to beat his ass, but that's it.

The tension is mounting on B yard. All the Hispanics are waiting to see how the Crips are going to respond. More and more Sureños are being told to all come outside. We know that when they get the order, they'll move as one disciplined unit.

As the day stretched on, the Hispanics saw we weren't taking any immediate action and got pissed off. They provoked an incident with this group of Bloods who had nothing to do with it and were playing handball on the court.

Their handball flew over a fence where the Sureños were sitting. They grabbed the ball and instead of throwing it back, they told the Bloods, "Fuck you."

The Bloods have no idea where this is coming from, and they start grouping up. All of us Crips start walking off the iron pile and met up with the Bloods to hear what happened.

"The Southsiders got our ball, they flipped us off, said, 'Fuck you' out of nowhere, we don't know what the fuck this is about. They blatantly disrespected us. We ain't having it."

A blown fuse. A *handball*, for fuck's sake.

Minor shit, but it's morphing into something major now. Something that's not going to be resolved by talking. The tension is getting heavier, because you got all the Crips on high alert, the Sureños on high alert, and now the Bloods feel disrespected. The police in the gun towers see something bad is brewing on B yard.

All the Sureños are outside, sitting on benches, not working out, not walking, not playing ball; they're waiting for the command from their shot-caller. Every single one of us who had some influence in our cars—all the different sets of Crips and Bloods—sent out the word that we're going to bring it to the Sureños' leadership before they can give the order to strike at us.

The various shot-callers decided that the Eight Trays and the Bloods were going to bring it to them, and the rest of us—all other Black inmates—would have their backs.

Their plan was to catch the Sureños shot-caller and all his lieutenants right when they were leaving the chow hall after breakfast. The next morning in the rotunda—the one passageway out of the line of sight of the gun towers—they caught the shot-caller and his people and stabbed them all. Then the stabbing also jumped off in the kitchen. The Bloods and Eight Trays had the element of surprise and got the better of the fighting. The gun towers started firing rubber bullets. The alarm sounded and everybody had to lie down.

In the final count, twenty-two dudes had to go to the hospital.

It was the worst-ever race riot at Calipatria.

We were immediately on lockdown. In retaliation for the attack on their shot-caller and his people, the Sureños gave out the order to kill one of us. The police know they can't even risk opening the gates, because the minute they do, the Sureños will send torpedoes to take out any Black dudes they can get close to.

The whole prison stays on lockdown while there's an investigation. You can't go to work. You don't get yard time. No phone calls or packages. You eat every meal in your cell. The only movement is when the police take you in handcuffs to the shower—and they might do that every three days. Six months locked in your six-by-nine cell, not going nowhere, everybody sweating and frustrated.

And during the state of emergency, all the hardship transfers are put on hold. They start dispersing various shot-callers from the Crips, Bloods, and Sureños who they determined instigated the violence.

A few of my homies from 30s were sent to Lancaster on buses. And immediately the rioting between Blacks and Hispanics jumped off there. The administration at Lancaster sends back word: *We don't want any more Blacks and Hispanics coming from Calipatria.* They don't want the violence to spread further.

Bottom line: because of the race riot, I never got my hardship transfer to Lancaster. Instead, as they continue shipping everybody out, they tell me I'm being bused to Centinela, which is forty-five minutes south, still in the Imperial Valley. At Centinela, the Hispanics outnumber the Blacks ten to one.

I'm really frustrated and pissed off because I'm no closer to my family—and I'm realizing that there's no way I'm going to see my dad before he dies. The very next day, they send me to the counselor's office. And we really got off to a bad start.

"Excuse me, ma'am, my name is Alton Pierce. I wanted to speak to you because I was granted a hardship transfer to Lancaster—"

"Lancaster is not accepting anybody," she said, not even bothering to look up from her paperwork.

"Yes, I know, ma'am, I'm trying to explain to you about my hardship—"

"Everybody's trying to get a hardship."

"You don't understand, ma'am. I was already *granted* a hardship."

She stared at me and snapped: "Look, you need to step outta my office."

I felt completely stuck, and my frustration kept building. I trusted my grandmother's faith when she asked God to watch over me, but the street dude inside of me was still trying to think of some way out. Every morning I'd wake up feeling like a wolf with his leg in a trap— desperately looking for any kind of wiggle room.

It's twisted, but this is the thinking of a real street motherfucker. Even though I'm guilty, even though I know I was the mastermind of this crime, I'm trying to find some angle so I can be released early and see my family somehow. In my mind, I'm still the slick-ass motherfucker who can manipulate things to his advantage.

I hadn't talked to my mom for a minute. I got on the phone in the dayroom at Centinela and started telling her about this wild scheme I had: if I could get one of the dudes who gave depositions against me to sign an affidavit, maybe I can get back into court for a new evidentiary hearing and get him to say something exculpatory—honestly, I was just rambling on, talking some far-fetched bullshit that was never going to happen.

My mother cut me off midsentence.

"Baby, be *quiet*! You're not in control anymore. God is in control. And God is going to get you out in *His* own time."

The power of her words knocked me back.

What did my mother just tell me?

It was the first time in my life that I ever remember my mother raising her voice to me. She was such a devout Christian lady. A painter. A children's book illustrator. She didn't drink, didn't smoke, didn't curse. Her demeanor was always calm and soft-spoken.

Anyone else could have said those same words to me and it wouldn't have made a bit of difference, but when my mother said it, I was speechless.

You're not in control anymore.

God is in control.

Honestly, it wasn't a message I wanted to hear.

But it was the message I needed to hear.

When I got off the phone, it resonated with me. I kept thinking about it. Days and months and years passed by. Even at this very moment, my mother's words echo in my mind.

The player-hustler that I perceived myself to be, that wasn't who my mother *raised* me to be. We were raised in the Baptist Church. I didn't lose my faith, but I wasn't serving God anymore.

I sat there in my cell, reflecting, reading passages of Scripture. I thought about Saul, on the road to Damascus, getting blinded by a vision of the Lord. The epiphany was so powerful that his heart changed. He submitted to serving God and became Saint Paul.

My mother didn't raise me to be doing all the destructive, negative things that landed me in prison, doing this life sentence.

I didn't have any compassion for society when I was coming up. None. From the time I was a teenager, my selfishness was supreme. My ego was out of control. Everything was about instant gratification.

I need to get this new Benz, I need to get this fly jewelry, I need to hit a million-dollar lick. . . .

All I cared about was me. I was out there in the streets taking shit and never thought about the ripple effects, all the different ways what I was doing was harming people. I didn't think that when I robbed somebody's store, maybe they had a child in the hospital and couldn't pay the bills because of what I took from them.

From the moment I accepted those words—"You're not in control anymore"—I knew I could never be the same man I was when I fell.

I had a long journey ahead of me—a difficult process of making that inner change—but it started there in my cell in Centinela with one realization.

I had to become my mother's son again.

ICE

Your ego and reality sometimes fight each other. Reality is staring you in the face, but your ego doesn't want to accept it.

We all go through it, in different ways, at different phases of our lives.

At the same time Spike was having to check his ego and accept certain hard truths about himself—facing up to the fact that his whole way of thinking about life, being a player and hustler, had led him nowhere—I was going through my own process of acceptance.

By the late '90s, I was at a crossroads. I wasn't in the best zone career-wise. My rap records weren't selling like they used to. My rock band was in tatters. I had my foot in the acting game, but I wasn't getting the greatest roles; I started doing all these low-budget B movies, rather than getting offers to do studio pictures. You can make a living acting in these cheaper movies that never get released in theaters—it might be a sixteen-day shoot and you still get a decent check. I mean, it'll keep your bills paid. I didn't really mind doing little low-budget films because I never looked at myself as a movie star. Acting was all just a hustle to me.

But the drop-off in my music sales—yeah, at first, that was a real fucking ego blow.

Most rappers or musicians who've tasted some success go through this same journey. Out the box, you're red fucking hot; all your concerts are selling out; you're making one hit record after the next. You feel kind of untouchable. And if you're lucky, you sustain that level for a while.

I had five straight gold albums—about a ten-year plateau—and then my sales just dropped off a steep fucking cliff. From being able to ship half a million records, suddenly I was only shipping 150,000. When I first realized it was happening, I took it personally, but that feeling lasted maybe two months. I noticed that it was the same story for Public Enemy, EPMD, Eric B. & Rakim. All these artists I respected were no longer selling like they used to. I said, "Okay, there's a paradigm shift going on. Hip-hop is transitioning to a new generation."

At the same time I was seeing my sales drop off, the whole vibe in rap had morphed into something darker. Pac and Biggie were dead. A bunch of cats who were selling well were on the precipice of disaster—getting shot, going to jail, involved in constant beef.

I didn't get into music to be caught up in street bullshit—just the opposite. I surveyed the scene and said, "Nah, I don't hustle backward. If I gotta get into drama to sell more records, then fuck it, I guess I ain't selling more records."

This was definitely not the place I wanted to be at when I was forty years old. I had to pause and reassess where I was headed.

One of the keys to my career longevity has been an awareness that there are times you need to humble yourself and simply switch lanes. You need to recognize that there are distinct phases to everything and be ready to embrace the changing phases.

Being orphaned by the time I was twelve, I didn't have a lot of time with my parents, so the things my mom and dad said to me are really imprinted on my mind.

My father was a real interesting cat. He fixed conveyor belts for a living. He was a blue-collar worker, but at night he dressed like a player. He put on his silk shirts and his gators to go out and do his thing, you know?

In the summertime I used to have a Kool-Aid stand set up in front of the house. A pitcher of Kool-Aid cost maybe a dollar and I'd sell glasses for a quarter apiece. I'd be able to make a profit of eight or nine bucks on a hot day. That was a nice little hustle for a youngster. But one day, the weather turned cold and nobody bought any Kool-Aid.

My pops came home and said, "How'd you do today?"

"It got cold—I didn't sell anything."

"Well, if they ain't buying Kool-Aid, sell 'em cookies."

He wasn't trying to give me a sweeping life lesson, but even today, I think about what my dad said—and it's fucking genius.

Don't let trends in the market affect your hustle.

As the game changes, you need to move and adapt. If the market suddenly switches up on you, don't get stuck—*pivot*.

In 1999, I got offered the chance to guest star on *Law & Order: SVU*. I was only booked for four episodes. It wasn't some big career change to me, just a gig so short-term that I was staying at a hotel in midtown Manhattan. But the producers liked my character, Odafin Tutuola, and they wanted to write more for him. They asked if I'd stay on for another year.

I agreed, mostly because I felt like my whole life was in limbo. By the end of the 1990s, my relationship was ending with the mom of my son, Little Ice. So I just picked up and left everything I had in

L.A. and transitioned to New York. I went from that big-ass house in Hollywood Hills and got a one-bedroom apartment with no furniture on West End Avenue. Left pretty much all my possessions and just came to New York to start over again.

I didn't know where this twist in my journey was going to take me. I mean, I didn't have a fucking crystal ball in 1999. I had no idea that I was going to be on *Law & Order* for more than twenty years and become the longest-running Black actor in TV history. I simply found myself in New York, in a better place, mentally, physically, emotionally.

Within a year, I'd met Coco, and that quickly turned into an amazing relationship—now a beautiful marriage, going strong more than twenty years.

When they gave me the part, the writers explained Fin's backstory. His parents were Black Panthers, and he'd gone to law school but decided to join the NYPD instead of becoming an attorney. But none of that shit was really helping me get into the character. Then Dick Wolf comes up to me. "Ice," he said, "you don't really like the cops, right?"

"Listen, cops are human beings. I ain't got problems with *all* cops. Some of 'em are assholes. Some of 'em are cool."

"So you admit we need the police, right?"

"Yeah."

"Okay," he says, "so play the cop we need."

I took that advice to heart. When you see me doing scenes as Fin, that's just Ice-T if he had ended up a cop. A decent, certified cat who happens to be an NYPD detective. All my scenes, all my lines, are filtered through my own experience and perspective.

When I started showing up on *Law & Order*, I remember cats like Spike sending us word that they were watching me in the pen. Dudes in prison used to say I was like Keyser Söze: hiding in plain sight. One of my player friends said, "Ice, you going from the streets to playing the police on TV is the biggest hustle in *history*, you know? You made the *ultimate* getaway."

SPIKE

In October 2000, I finally received my hardship transfer to Donovan State Prison in San Diego. But it was too late for me to see my father. His cancer had progressed and there was no way he could make the 120-mile trip from L.A. to San Diego. My dad died on September 25, 2002, without us ever getting a chance to see each other face-to-face again.

At Donovan, I joined Kairos, a prison-based ministry group, and attended church regularly. Kairos—that's Greek for "God's Time"—became an integral part of my life. Eventually, I began lecturing there as well. Kairos was crucial in helping me cope with the grief and loss within my family—once again, helping me see the ripple effects of my bad decisions.

Mostly what I did at Donovan was work. There's a big commercial laundry in the prison servicing all these Veterans Administration hospitals and local prisons, and I got a full-time job in there paying me about thirty cents an hour.

When I wasn't working in the laundry, I started writing and recording songs. This dude I met had a little cassette recorder, and over the years I recorded something like sixty songs. I studied all the rappers I loved and really analyzed and broke down how they created their flows, their similes and metaphors, the way they told stories. I wanted to emulate that. The more I studied, the more I honed my own craft.

I realized it was too late for me to ever have a career as a recording artist, but I thought if I kept polishing my skills maybe I could be a ghostwriter for some other artists someday. I have a song called "Salt of the Earth" that really breaks down what I was feeling at the time in prison:

Trapped in our fate
Like a soul in a fuckin' crate
Heaven or hell's entrance gates
Blocked with yellow tape
Accusing God for our psychological sabotage
Searching for loopholes in a law
Cloaked in camouflage
And prison walls be our destinies
"Help us Lord!"
Sentenced to life, still plottin'
Tryin' to get it all
Are we insane?
Or just too caught up in the fuckin' game?

During my years at Donovan, I was on the road to change—really committed to becoming my mother's son again. I was committed to getting down to a Level II, where I could at least have a chance of making parole.

In all my choices, in all my decisions, I started to ask myself, "What would my mother have me do?"

All the time that I was in prison, I only had one family visit. I saw my mother and daughter one time. My nephew drove them the 120 miles from L.A. to San Diego to see me at Donovan.

When I fell, my daughter was seven; when she walked into the visiting room she was a fully grown woman in her twenties, and I could see how she was emotionally scarred by my absence from her life during those crucial teenage years. The damage was apparent, but at least there was some hope of rebuilding.

The change in my mother was even more shocking to me. And there was no fixing it. My mother was suffering from Alzheimer's—nobody in my family had told me. During our visit she kept looking over her shoulder quickly. Like something in the room was frightening her or someone was talking to her. I didn't understand at the time that it was dementia taking hold of her thoughts. She kept holding my hand and telling me I hadn't changed a bit in more than fifteen years, but at times it was like she didn't realize what had happened to bring me to prison. At times she'd be speaking to me as if I were still a ten-year-old boy.

As grateful as I was to see my mom and my daughter, it was also heartbreaking. People who've had a parent or loved one experience the deterioration of Alzheimer's understand. I was physically sitting with my mother, but mentally she was no longer the same woman I'd known out in the free world.

As far as Ice goes, I hadn't been able to get in touch with him in years. His numbers had all changed—I couldn't call him at his office anymore. I was really in the dark. At one point, Trome mailed me some photos of an event they'd been at out in Las Vegas. Ice got this lifetime achievement award at our friend Michael Carter's Players Toast. There was a snapshot of Ice with his silver Bentley Continental GT Coupe. There was one of Ice, onstage in a gray suit, looking superfly, while Trome's handing him this trophy that looks like a giant diamond. Trome's wearing a silk suit and he looks like money, man! Michael Carter, Sean E. Sean, all of the close crew were suited up and looked like they were having a blast.

Damn, I thought, *I definitely should have been there.*

I knew the lifetime achievement award must have meant a whole lot to Ice, because it was coming from the original crew, from his friends, the real players who knew him before fame. I stared at those photos for hours. I read the words from Trome over and over: "We miss you, Spike, we love you." When you get any kind of letter or photos from home and you're doing a life sentence, you treasure every word, you hang on to every word—every single word feels like a lifeline.

I finally reached out through Trome and Cousin Rich and got caught up. That was the first time I learned about Ice relocating to New York City and starting a new job on *Law & Order.*

Seeing Ice every week on *Law & Order* was one of my biggest motivations to keep striving to better myself. I didn't tell any of the dudes I was locked up with about how I used to run with Ice, how we used to hit licks together, or that I was part of the Rhyme Syndicate, touring the country with him. But even watching that show in silence really boosted my sense of pride that one of my closest friends had stuck to his word, had consistently stayed true to himself, showing that with hard work and persistence any goals were reachable.

Listen, when we were young, Ice was just as bad as any motherfucker I knew in that crime world, but he made the right decision when he became legit. He then left that shit behind and changed his life, continuously making good decisions. He'd turned his life around completely. Now every week I'd see him on TV as Fin, this smooth-looking detective, and say, "No matter who you used to be, or what you used to be, *anyone* can transform themselves."

Besides inspiration, it gave me *courage*. Courage to seek real change in whatever direction my new life took.

I remember writing a letter to Ice that first season he was on *Law & Order.*

"Man, you're the *only* cop that the cats inside cheer for."

ICE

When I moved to New York, I really tightened up my circle. I set a limit on the people I communicated with daily. In L.A., everyone knew they could find me at my office in Hollywood. Over the years that led to a bunch of problems—some crazy street drama—and since I was starting fresh in New York, I took the opportunity to be real selective about who I allowed in my inner circle.

Working full-time on a network TV show can mean long hours. A lot of days you're on set 7 a.m. to 7 p.m., shooting on location, and you can't be getting fucking calls throughout the day.

At the time, Spike was one of about ten homies I had doing time, either in federal or state prisons. All of them used to call me on a regular basis. Right around this time, dudes started to have cell phones smuggled inside. That was a game-changer. In prison it's a lifeline—it's the only way cats can talk to people on the outside without standing at some wall for fifteen minutes with the cops monitoring every word. Most of the guys don't use the contraband phones for anything criminal—it's just a way they can stay sane by talking to their family and friends in a semi-relaxed way.

But being in my position, that created a new level of risk. You've got to realize that a bunch of random dudes in prison could be paying to use the same cell phone. And if the C.O.s discover it, all they need to do is backtrack all the numbers in the call history. Some dude that I don't even know may have committed a crime on the inside and then the cops find out he used the same cell phone that one of my friends used to call me. Next thing you know the news will be saying, *"Law & Order* actor Ice-T" is mixed up with some bullshit I had nothing to do with.

I said to myself, *I'm just trying to get on my feet in New York, start a new chapter in my life, and I don't need any extra drama.*

I made a decision: I wasn't talking directly to anybody on the inside. No calls from prison. Not even from Spike, and he's like a brother to me. I wanted them to be able to reach out, but I needed a buffer. We came up with a system, one we still use today. Everything related to our dudes in prison goes through Al Patrome. Technically, Al P.'s my road manager, but unofficially we gave him a new title: head of inmate affairs.

Al P. keeps one designated number that our friends inside can call. He talks to them, filters the conversations, and if there's an important issue he relays the message to me. Some dudes need money for a lawyer, some dudes need money for their commissary, some have family problems on the outside and they want us to help.

From my perspective, from my end of the phone call, it's always a long-ass speech full of explanations and pleading that ends up with some variation of "Here's what I need . . ."

I told Al P., "Look, cut to the chase. Ask them from the jump, 'What do you *need?*'"

It's almost always financial. And I've got no problem looking out. I'd much rather help a motherfucker who's in jail than a dude in the street. Once you're in the street, it's on you. My attitude is: *Look, you're free. Go get your hustle on.*

But sometimes it's not money; it's literally just a human connection. A pen pal. Somebody who's willing to listen to you. Or do some little routine things for you on the outside. When we first got reconnected back to Spike—I guess he was still in Calipatria in the mid-1990s—he sent us some pictures of himself out on the yard, on swole, wearing braids, looking wild. He asked us to find him a girl who would write to him.

A lot of times when you're in jail you need a girl to run for you. Guys won't run for you; they count you for dead. But a girl, if she has feelings for you, she'll be like a prison wife. She'll run around and do all the shit you need done while you're stuck in there.

I'll never forget this hilarious shit that happened one time when we were out on tour with Body Count. All these chicks were jocking us and I kept saying, "Yo, don't jock us. Why don't you write to my man Spike? He's stuck right now." And we'd show his prison pictures.

"Oh, he's a handsome brother."

Al P. gave out the info to this one chick we met on tour, and she started to write Spike and accept his collect calls from inside.

But a few weeks after the tour, this call comes in at the office from Spike:

"Tell Ice I need another broad."

I got on the line: "Spike, didn't we just hook you up? We got you a fine-looking bitch, man. What happened?"

"Ice, man, that chick was always telling me about *her* problems! I'm in *prison*. I'm in this Level IV dungeon and all she wants to do is complain. I couldn't listen anymore—I had to cut her off. That chick has more problems than *me*!"

The truth is, when you're behind bars, you can really only help yourself so much. This is the dilemma for a lot of guys. They're stuck, physically and mentally. They know their position is fucked up, but they can't see a way to maneuver their way out. Nothing you can do on the outside is going to help them.

If they stay in there and keep acting up—stabbing motherfuckers, fighting with C.O.s, getting thrown in the hole—there's nothing we can do from the outside. There's no amount of money that can get you out of prison if you keep getting caught up in more bullshit. You have to put yourself in the right position to get a date before that parole board.

Then, maybe, we can help you to make the case that you're a changed man.

That's the message we kept relaying to Spike. "Listen, man, just get yourself to the point where we can actually help you. When you get yourself a date before the board, we'll pay for an attorney. You ain't going in there with a public defender. But you need to do the heavy lifting first. *You* need to put yourself in a position where we can help you get a shot at freedom."

I mean, I've known a lot of dudes who did time. And everybody's prison journey is different. Spike had such a long sentence—thirty-five to life—I think for the first ten years he pretty much had to become a monster. No way he could even think about rehabilitation right out the gate: he had to go straight into that survival-of-the-fittest mode. He had to adopt that institutionalized mentality. Hitting the weight pile. Taking no bullshit. Not for the sake of being a badass, but just to keep dudes from fucking with you.

And once you can establish a rep, once dudes are leaving you alone, then you can work on lowering your classification, bettering yourself, going to school, taking the self-help classes, doing your time productively.

What I found real interesting is all these guys in my circle would go to jail and they'd get no help from anybody else. Literally none. It was always the same story. I was their *only* friend. Some of these cats have huge families and I was the only guy helping. Me—the guy with *no* family. The guy who grew up in South Central as an orphan.

A lot of dudes were surrounded by a gang of motherfuckers when they were running the streets, driving expensive whips, making serious paper, but I was their only friend when the chips were down. I didn't mind it. If I had the wherewithal to help, why the fuck wouldn't I? But I'd always tell them, "Get a good look at this shit. You might want to remember some of these folks who went AWOL on you when you were stuck."

That's a cold, hard lesson prison teaches you.

You won't know who's *really* got your back until you're up against it.

CHAPTER 12

A LICK FOR MY LIFE

Make parole
Meant I had to hit a lick for my life
Write and recite, sharpen skills, like prison-made knife
Told myself, never to die inside the muthafuckin' fence
Wrote some bomb shit
Lyrics defy worst fuckin' critics
Five mics ain't hard to write,
When facing 35 to life
No date in sight
Up against it like Passion of the Christ

—SPIKE, "OUTSIDE LOOKING IN"

SPIKE

In late 2007, I found out I was being transferred out of Donovan, to a different Level III at Ironwood. The night before the transfer, a letter from my daughter arrived in the late mail. It was December 14, 2007, my birthday. All my property was already packed and I was getting on a bus first thing in the morning. In the letter, my daughter wrote, "Sorry about what happened to your brother Robert."

I didn't even understand what she was talking about. I had to wait until I got settled in at Ironwood and was allowed to make a phone call. My daughter told me that my brother Robert was dead.

Robert, my closest brother, had died in prison—the story she heard was that he'd had a complication from some medications and had a heart attack. The coldest part is that he'd been dead and buried for two months—nobody besides my daughter had thought to tell me about it!

Again, that's how death comes to you in prison. It only accentuates the feeling of being trapped and powerless and cut off from the rest of the world.

There was nothing I could do but pray for Robert.

In the next few months, I was sent to four different prisons—Ironwood, North Kern, Pleasant Valley, and finally Corcoran. One thing about doing a long sentence is you don't want to get comfortable but you do want to have a settled routine so you can do your time productively. That's tough when you're moving constantly from one prison to the next, getting to know new inmates, counselors, and cops.

But I see now it was a necessary part of my journey—my points kept dropping until I was eligible for a Level II yard, and they had to find a suitable place for me. Corcoran was the place that God intended for me, the place where I could fully embrace and manifest the change I needed to make.

Because it was at Corcoran—on the Level II yard—that I immediately ran across some guys I'd known in L.A., and they changed my whole outlook on doing time. There was this one guy in particular; his name was Rafik. He'd known me since I was in high school. He'd been a hustler, a player, a stone-cold street dude just like me. But in prison he became a Muslim. I always saw him walking around with college books. I couldn't believe how much he'd changed—his whole demeanor and mentality, outwardly and inwardly. He was clean-cut. Wearing glasses. Carrying himself with dignity, like a real man should.

"Spike, listen," Rafik said, "you should take advantage of all the stuff they've got here." He told me about the various college courses he was enrolled in. He was involved with the Scared Straight program and various other inmate self-helps.

Besides Rafik, I met a bunch of dudes who were getting themselves together—guys who'd already done twenty or thirty years on their life sentences. I realized it was a whole different mindset on a Level II yard. You've got much more freedom of movement. You live in dorms. Daily life wasn't so much about prison politics, racial tensions, and constantly watching your back.

Everyone I knew was focusing on bettering themselves and doing the necessary things required if they were going to get paroled. I said, "Damn, I better have something to take before the board. I need to start getting my ducks in a row."

Before enrolling in college, I started knocking down all kinds of trades. Electronics technician. Fiber optics. Masonry. Plumbing. Janitorial. I was learning trades I never thought I'd be interested in doing out in the free world, but I wanted to bring in certificates of fully completed classes. I wanted to show the board that I was applying myself to change. I wanted them to see that I had the training and desire to work an honest job out in the world.

Once I had every trade certificate I could get at Corcoran, I enrolled in a two-year college program. It had been so long since my last stint in college, but my aptitude for academics came back to me quickly.

I was enrolled in four or five courses each semester—classes in psychology, sociology, world history, American history. The way I used to bust down and do my exercise, I would do the same thing mentally with my college work. I'd get up very early in the morning, before breakfast, and put in two hours of studying my lessons, writing essays, prepping for the quizzes and exams. When my grades came in, they were mostly A's and B's, and I was proud that I'd made the dean's honors list.

Every morning, before I started schoolwork, I thought about my grandmother's dying wish that I humble myself and submit myself wholeheartedly to God's will and be subservient to His word. And each day, as she'd asked, I read passages of Scripture. I sincerely tried to change the nature of my heart and ask the Lord to intercede on my behalf.

For years, I was involved in the inmate self-help programs at Corcoran: Alternatives to Violence. Restorative Justice. Criminals and Gang Members Anonymous. Anger Management. I joined Alcoholics Anonymous and Narcotics Anonymous—even though I never drank or did drugs myself, I had an older brother whose demise was drugs; I had an uncle who drank himself to death. Eventually, I became a certified substance-abuse counselor.

I wanted to learn everything I could about the faces of addiction. I wanted to understand all the ripple effects of crime and violence. I began running workshops dealing with nonviolent conflict resolution.

And besides running inmate self-helps, in 2009 I got involved in the Scared Straight program at Corcoran, and before long, I was one of the trainers. The officers would bring a group of about twenty kids to the fence, where I'd meet them with a group of other lifers.

"Mr. Pierce, how are you doing today?" the captain says. "I got twenty little juvenile delinquents and I don't want them in my prison. Can I turn them over to you? This is your yard, right?"

"Yes, captain. Open the fence and let these kids on my yard."

I didn't care much for all that screaming that the police do—the "scared" part of the program. These kids are a lot smarter than we give them credit for. They know already that the prisoners can't do anything physically threatening or endangering that would result in a lawsuit. That part was totally theatrical, and the more streetwise kids know that already.

My strength in running that program wasn't instilling fear. It was more about the straight talk. I didn't bullshit. I'd have them all lined up in the hot sun.

"I'm going to be honest with you," I'd say. "I'm not here to save *all* of you. Because no matter what we say or do, some of you *are* going to end up here. And some of you are probably going to die in those streets. But maybe there are some of you guys who are smart enough to avoid coming to this motherfucking place, because we damn sure don't want you here."

For seven years, I did this with hundreds and hundreds of kids. In a couple of hours, you give them a taste of prison. You show them what it feels like to be locked in a cell. You show them what it's like to have to eat a lunch of nasty prison bologna in ten minutes before your ass is ordered to get up and leave the chow hall. All of that is supposed to give them a real-world feeling for prison.

To me, the most important stage was the last part of the tour, where we broke up into one-on-ones and became active listeners.

For most of them, dysfunction has become the norm. Some of these kids come from families where every man—fathers, brothers, uncles, cousins—is a gang member. Or they didn't know their dad—maybe he was a lifer himself, or he was a pimp or a hustler out in the streets.

I'd always focus on that one kid who was acting like a tough guy or rolling his eyes like he don't give a fuck—because deep down, I can see that his self-esteem is shit. You're dealing with a little wannabe gangster with his chest puffed out, but instead of scaring him, you want to establish a connection—let him see that you actually care about what he's going through.

"I was once you," I would say. "Believe me, homie, you *don't* want to be me."

In those one-on-ones, if you're lucky, you make a real human connection. You tell them how you acted when you were their age—whether it was stealing cars, smoking weed, whatever. Once you establish that connection, it's amazing what you hear. I had kids spill their guts and tell me stuff they wouldn't tell their parents or even their friends.

"Listen, homie, you're only fifteen. You can curb this. You have choices. You have options. You don't have to end up here."

With some kids, you could still see a glimpse of the innocence buried in there someplace. Because before the streets became their surrogate parents, everybody had innocent dreams. Everybody wanted to be something: firefighter, veterinarian, scientist.

"Listen, I had a chance to be something, man. When I was your age, I was a star baseball player. Sitting here in prison, I've seen people on TV that I played against in high school. They're in the major leagues—why the fuck am I locked up here at Corcoran? Because I was stupid, man. I was immature, I was selfish, I made bad choices, man. I made so many bad choices! You don't have to make those choices, man."

I'd be real transparent with them. "Yeah, I had dreams of being a professional baseball player. Or a rapper, touring the world. You want to know what my dream is now? I've just got one dream: to die on the other side of the electric fence."

One afternoon, they called me into the warden's office at Corcoran. The warden wanted to talk to me personally. I was nervous, because in more than twenty years of prison, I'd never been called into the warden's office. I walked in and he smiled at me, handing me a letter. It was from a fifteen-year-old Mexican American kid named Danny who I'd tried to connect with in a one-on-one.

This prison visit was a great eye-opener for me. There was a metaphor that one of the prisoners used. He told me there are two dogs inside me, a good one and a bad one. "Who do you think will win in a fight? The one you feed more." That saying stuck with me because it shows that it all depends on what we do. If you do bad things, the bad dog is going to win. I need to feed my good dog and starve my bad dog. I need to start doing more good things and less bad things in my daily routine.

That was one of the main visualization lessons I used to give the kids. We've all got that good and bad dog inside of us, tearing at each other, and it's up to us which dog to feed and which to starve—and we do that through every single daily decision we make in our lives.

The whole time I was in Corcoran, I was constantly thinking about the parole board, but it was still a mystery to me. There were so many guys I came across in prison who were like Rafik: they seemed to be model prisoners, finished college, taking all the self-helps, doing outreach with at-risk juveniles. These guys were impressive and visibly changed—yet they'd hit a roadblock at the board.

They used to tell me that trying to figure out a parole board hearing was like solving a Rubik's cube. You might get ninety-nine answers out of a hundred right, but with that one wrong answer you'll hear: "Denied. We'll holler at you in another seven to fifteen years."

Unless you got hit with LWOP, there's a date calculated when you're first eligible for a parole hearing. Doesn't mean you'll actually get that hearing, but it's your first eligible date. Mine was December 5, 2013. Everyone kept telling me that given the amount of time I'd been sentenced to and the nature of my crime—and all the publicity surrounding it in San Diego—I should expect a denial of five years.

But I didn't accept that. I was intent on showing my transformation at the initial suitability hearing.

I knew it wasn't going to be easy. I had to do everything possible to convince the parole board I was a changed man. I had to use all my willpower, wits, and creativity—skills I misused in the streets—to prove myself.

Changing my heart and demonstrating that change was the most important work I would ever do.

I had to hit a final lick for my life.

By 2009, I hadn't talked directly to Ice in more than ten years. I was only calling Trome to check in from time to time.

That idea of using a buffer was still foreign to me—I was still wrapping my head around the idea that Ice wasn't talking to nobody on cell phones. Then in the summer of 2009, Al Patrome did something that was so crucial to me. It was a small gesture, but I'll appreciate it for the rest of my life.

I told Trome that I really wanted to convey something to Ice personally. Voice to voice. I wanted him to hear the inner changes I was making. Trome thought about it for a while, then he said, "Look, Spike, I'm going to make it happen. Just this one time, I want to get this phone to Ice's ear for you."

He was in L.A. but was about to fly to New York to be with Ice for a concert in Manhattan. He gave me a specific time the next day to call back. I did, and he told me to hold the line. I could hear him going through a hotel lobby, talking to security, explaining that he was Ice-T's road manager.

He walked into a hotel room, there was some chatter, then he put his own Bluetooth piece right on Ice's ear.

"Spike?"

"What's up, Ice?"

"Shit, good to hear your voice, man! Welcome back to the family."

"Man, listen, I've been trying to talk to you for the longest. But Trome and them were telling me they couldn't even hand you the phone."

"Yeah, I got them doing that," he said. "Don't even trip. There's a lot of shit been going on and I'm just not talking to people on the phone like I used to. It has nothing to do with you. Spike, you've never crossed me. You'll always be part of the family."

"Listen, man," I said, "I just wanted to let you know I'm in a Level II yard and I'm doing everything I need to do to get ready for that board."

I told him about working on my college degree, running the Scared Straight program and a bunch of inmate self-help groups. It was a short call but I wanted to convey to Ice personally how intensely I was committed to change.

"That's what we want to hear, Spike," Ice said. "Keep pushing, man. Keep doing what you're doing. Stay in touch with Al P., and we'll be there to help you when you come before the board."

Long before my initial parole suitability hearing, I did the legwork and found an attorney in Oakland named Keith Watley. He was considered one of the best in the state at handling parole boards.

I didn't have the kind of money it was going to cost to retain him, and no one in my family was in a position to help. But Ice was true to his word; he stepped up to help financially. Keith Watley came down from Oakland five times to meet with me at Corcoran. Most guys have a court-appointed attorney who they meet once, briefly, a few days before the hearing.

The most valuable thing you get from a good private attorney is a full understanding of the obstacles you're facing at the board hearing. The attorney can't do the hard work for you. You've got to bring the board years of proof that you're working on change: certificates showing that you've learned various trades, been going to college, doing self-helps. Your disciplinary record has to speak for itself. You better not any have any 115s—those are administrative write-ups for infractions in prison. Even during the hearing, your lawyer might only talk for fifteen minutes. The rest is on you.

But he can prepare you by helping you understand strategy. One thing I learned is that the parole board is looking for you to tell the story of your life—your personal narrative—in a compelling way.

"Go in there and tell them your story," Keith Watley said. "Tell them why you committed the crime. And the number one thing is this: keep it one hundred percent real. Don't lie about anything. Don't downplay anything. Don't minimize anything. Minimization is the main issue the board looks for."

He told me that if they felt I was minimizing even *one* aspect of the crime, I'd be lucky to walk away with a five-year denial.

"Listen, you've got to put your head on the chopping block," he said. "You've got to cut your own head off before they do."

In other words, I needed to own up to all my mistakes and flaws and bad decisions before the commissioners could even ask me about them.

I needed to describe—in detail—the kind of person I was back then. I had to tear down everything I'd built up over the years: my justifications, rationalizations, all my defense mechanisms. I had to *own* those bad choices. I couldn't point the finger at anyone but myself.

In the months I spent preparing for the hearing, I took a moral inventory and accepted that I'd allowed myself to become a twisted, self-centered individual who didn't stop to think about the ripple effects of any of my actions.

But now I was nearly fifty years old; I was no longer the same selfish, reckless young player I had been in my twenties. I needed to differentiate between the person who committed those crimes and the person who was coming to the board hoping to be granted a second chance at freedom. The commissioners didn't want to see the Spike who was apprehended in 1992 and convicted at trial of first-degree murder.

They needed to see my mother's son.

Keith Watley warned me that this would be one of most intimidating experiences of my life. And that was the truth—my initial hearing lasted ten hours. They came and got me at 8 a.m. We assembled in a small conference room at Corcoran. Right in front of me, I was staring at a panel of three commissioners from Sacramento; on my left side, there was a district attorney from San Diego and Keith Watley; and on my right side, several members of the victim's family.

These commissioners are former judges and cops—they can read your expressions and your body language. They can tell if you're being sincere in your responses or bullshitting them and just telling them what they want to hear.

"Mr. Pierce, you were the ringleader. You could have gone in there and just taken the jewelry. Why didn't you?"

"Mr. Commissioner, I didn't usually commit robberies this way, using guns. I usually robbed stores using the element of surprise. I'd break the glass using just a hammer. But on that day in May 1992, I made that bad decision to involve a group of people who wanted to use guns, because that was their method of robbery."

I told the commissioners, "That was the manner of person I was back then. Today, twenty-one years later, that's not the same person you see sitting before you."

For hours they dissected every aspect of the planning and execution of the crime. We went through all the numerous times when I could have stopped it.

One commissioner wanted to know why I'd joined Alcoholics Anonymous and Narcotics Anonymous:

"Mr. Pierce, you weren't involved in drugs and alcohol?"

"No, but I realized I was living the life of criminality at a level that was an addiction," I said. "My life of criminality was my addiction. Not just the robbing, but the womanizing . . . doing things that wasn't legal. Any time you rob, you steal, you disrespect someone in any capacity, all that falls, to me, under 'criminality.' I needed help in that area. These self-helps like N.A. made me understand why I needed God to change me. I couldn't do it by myself."

The panel wanted to know why I'd orchestrated the robberies in La Jolla—besides the allure of "fast money." They asked me to nail down the "causative factors" that had driven me toward criminality.

"My low self-esteem," I said. "My impulsive decision-making, greed, laziness, selfishness."

They asked me about my inherent sense of right and wrong. I told them I always had a sense of right and wrong. But the manner of person I was back then, I was conditioned to being reckless and selfish, and I wasn't listening to my conscience telling me that what I was doing was wrong.

I apologized to the victim's family; I admitted that even though I didn't shoot him, I was truly the person responsible for him losing his life:

"I regret every moment that I didn't stop this crime from happening. And I know I destroyed his family. I took away his chance to live, his chance to be a father, a parent, a grandfather, watch his unborn kids grow. I know I took away his chance to continue to love his wife—a widow because of me. I know I set all these things in motion. . . . I took so much from that family, I took a part of everybody that loved him, a piece of everyone that loved him, and that haunts me every day because I'm ashamed of myself and I'm guilty of it. And not a day goes by that I don't think about it. For the rest of my life, until I die, that's going to be part of my life."

However, I stressed that I wasn't the same person I was when I committed the crime. "I've changed," I said. "I've changed my value system, my beliefs. I've worked hard, through behavioral rehabilitation and therapy, twelve-steps, and my everyday life. I know I have the confidence to do things that are necessary for me to be a contributor to society in a positive way. That's the way I would like to be remembered—as someone who made the change under these circumstances that I brought on myself."

When we adjourned and the commissioners deliberated, the police took me back to a holding cell. My attorney told me he thought I'd handled that ten-hour hearing as well as anyone could have handled it, but he said the most likely outcome was a denial—maybe three years. Maybe five. Maybe seven.

They called us back into the room and told us their decision. They believed that I had changed and my record indicated I'd been a model inmate. They felt I was no longer a safety risk to society and found me suitable for parole.

Almost immediately, the San Diego DA wrote the governor's office appealing the finding of suitability. The DA argued that I still posed a significant risk to public safety. The victim's family were also strongly opposed to my being released.

It was eighteen months later before we had a second hearing. The first question the commissioners asked me was how I felt about being at this appeal hearing, how I felt about my release date being taken away. I knew they were judging my body language, trying to see if I would maintain my composure.

"I feel like I'm a changed man," I said. "But if the board feels like I haven't changed, then I don't *want* to go home. I don't *want* you to release me. Because I've done everything that I can possibly do to demonstrate the change. If you feel I haven't changed sufficiently, I'd ask you, 'What else do you want me to do?'"

The main question I had to address was the DA's assertion that I failed to understand the "natural and probable consequences" of my actions. Murder was not my intent when planning the robberies in La Jolla. But that doesn't matter in the eyes of the law.

"Because my accomplices were using guns in a crime that I planned," I said, "I should have recognized that there was a reasonable probability that someone would get shot and killed during the commission of that crime. And, tragically, that was the case."

They grilled me back and forth for hours and then, after a recess, the commissioners called us back in. "Based on our findings, we feel that Mr. Pierce would no longer pose an unreasonable risk to society, and we do find him suitable for parole."

I shook Keith Watley's hand, but I wasn't about to celebrate. He'd already explained to me that there's another 120-day waiting period. Even though I'd twice been found suitable and granted parole, if there was enough political pressure, the governor could overrule the board with one stroke of the pen. When it comes to murder cases in California, that's the law.

It was the afternoon of January 7, 2016, more than three years since my first parole hearing. I wasn't expecting to go free anytime soon.

Actually, I was bracing myself for a denial. I figured I'd get the news in the mail saying that Governor Jerry Brown had overturned my suitability and I would need to come before the board in another five or seven years.

If that was the case, I had to accept it. I had to trust my mother's words:

God will get you out in His time.

That afternoon the alarms went off and we went into lockdown. The cops were searching all the dorms for contraband—especially cell phones and drugs. They stripped us down to our boxers and took us out of our building. We were all inside of a kitchen, with the police up in the gun tower watching everybody—Blacks, whites, Hispanics—all out there together wearing only our shower shoes and underwear.

In the middle of the search, I heard over the loudspeaker:

"Pierce, report to the counselor's office."

I looked at one of the cops. "How can I go to the counselor's office? I ain't wearing no pants!"

A couple of the riot-squad police came and took me back to get a shirt and pair of pants, and they accompanied me to the programs office. My counselor was a young Hispanic woman, Ms. Lopez; she was fairly new at Corcoran, and I'd only dealt with her once or twice. When I walked in, she was staring at some paperwork on her desk.

"How are you doing, Mr. Pierce?" she said.

"I'm fine, ma'am."

"How do you feel about going home?"

I wasn't sure I'd heard correctly so I asked, "How do I feel about what?"

"Mr. Pierce, you're going home tomorrow."

"Are you serious?"

She explained that Governor Brown had signed the order offi-cially granting me parole: January 8, 2016, was my release date.

For a long time, I couldn't even speak. Tears were streaming down my cheeks.

"Mr. Pierce, I'm happy for you," she said, smiling. "You've worked very hard to make this happen."

The police led me back to the chow hall. Everyone was asking me what was going on, why I was wearing clothes, but I couldn't tell them the truth—*I'm going home tomorrow!* First of all, it was hard for me to believe. I was still in shock. I kept feeling the rug might be snatched out from under me. Second of all, some of these guys have been denied two or three times, and I didn't want them to feel fucked up that I was granted parole at my first suitability hear-ing. Because from everything I heard, that almost *never* happens to someone with a life sentence.

It might have been the strangest night I ever spent during all my years in prison. I couldn't fall asleep for even a minute. I was too excited about the idea of going free. But also, I was still not believing it. I lay on top of my bed, eyes wide open, fully dressed.

In the morning, I looked outside and it was a cold, foggy day. Another announcement came over the loudspeakers.

"Pierce, report to the back gate."

I gave all my belongings to one of my homies: TV, books, clothes, shoes. I didn't want to carry anything with me except my daughter's pictures, my photo albums of the Syndicate, my legal paperwork, and important letters—especially the one my grandmother wrote on her deathbed.

As I was leaving the dorm, there was bounce in my stride. Someone shouted to me:

"You goin' home, Spike?"

"Hell yeah—I'm going home."

Now the whole building started clapping.

I got outside and the fog was so thick I couldn't see ten feet in front of my face. I was sipping from a can of orange soda and walking past the police with a smile.

"Pierce, you're going home?"

"Yes, I am, sir."

"Good for you, Pierce. Congratulations."

There was a prison van waiting to take me to a train station. They had already bought me the tickets on Amtrak going to Bakersfield and then on Greyhound to L.A. They waited with me at the station and physically escorted me to my seat on the train. I'd never been on an Amtrak in my life. Everything was new and modern, and it felt like I was on a spaceship—everybody was staring at their iPads and smartphones and talking to themselves. It took me a while to understand they were on Bluetooth earpieces.

I was glued to my seat like a kid on a field trip, taking it all in. I got off at Bakersfield, transferred to a Greyhound, and got down to Union Station in L.A. It was swarming with people rushing everywhere. I stopped someone to ask for directions to where I was heading in downtown L.A.

"You need to take the blue line to the red line . . ."

Man, I didn't know anything about blue lines and red lines! I'd never been on the L.A. subway system. But I managed to find my way down to this transitional housing place called Amity, on Grand and Thirty-Seventh Street. My first meal there, I immediately got really sick. Jail food and what we call "street food"— food out in the free world—aren't the same. I'd been eating jail food for so many years, my system couldn't handle the richness of street food.

The staff sent me to a clinic on Skid Row to get some medication. I had to take a bus there, and this older Hispanic dude who'd paroled out a few months earlier came with me; he was kind of like a chaperone, since I was feeling so sick and it was my first day on the street.

He was a pretty cool dude and he had a little cell phone, which he let me use once we were in the waiting room at the clinic. My first call was to Trome. I didn't even let him know I was back on the streets.

"Who's this?" He didn't recognize the number on the caller ID.

"Hey, Trome, it's Spike. What's going on?"

"Hey, Spike, what's happening up there?" He was talking real nonchalant, since he thinks I'm still on the prison yard.

"Listen, man, I'm staying at this place downtown but my stomach's all fucked up and I'm trying to get me some medicine—"

"Wait, what? Downtown? You're *out*?"

"Yeah, nigga, I'm out!"

"You bullshittin', Spike!"

"Nigga, I'm out. I'm down here on Skid Row at a clinic that these people sent me to."

Straightaway he says, "Give me the motherfucking address, I'll put it in the GPS. Don't leave that clinic, Spike."

He dropped everything he was doing. I was sitting there in the middle of a waiting room and thirty minutes later, Trome pulled up in his white Mercedes-AMG, going the wrong way on a one-way street. Just left his car there in the street, rushed inside with a few other dudes. We had all gotten so much older, I didn't even realize that it was two of my homies from the 30s, Michael Cansler and Terry Cansler.

They all ran in and hugged me at the same time—it almost felt like I was being tackled. We just stood there in the clinic, a bunch of grown-ass men with gray hair—huddled together, crying together. Then Cousin Rich and his son showed up and started hugging me and crying, too. I hadn't seen Rich in more than twenty years, and it was my first time meeting his son.

You see, that's Trome's get-down; in less than thirty minutes he had let all these dudes know the news, and it was a mob scene in that clinic. There was so much emotion because none of them could believe I was really free.

The security guard was a middle-aged Black lady and I heard her saying under her breath, "Whoever this dude is, they *love* him."

We were making so much commotion that we needed to take it out into the street. The clinic was on a rough block—we had to side-step a bunch of homeless dudes lying there. I was just trying to get my bearings, trying to believe all this was actually happening.

"Hold on, hold on," Trome said, and next thing you know he was making a video call to somebody. At first, I didn't even realize that he was talking to Ice in New York.

"There's proof of life," Trome said.

"Proof of life? What the fuck—"

"Spike hit the bricks."

"What! My nigga's *home*? For real?"

Trome turned the phone around so we could see each other.

"Spike, man, you really out? You're really home?"

Ice had a big smile, and it looked like he had tears in his eyes.

"Yeah, Ice," I said, wiping my own eyes with the back of my hand. "I'm really home."

EPILOGUE

SPLIT DECISION

The homies came back from the pen
And we all worked together
True friends

—ICE, *"THAT'S HOW I'M LIVIN'"*

ICE

When we saw each other on that video call, for me, honestly, it was like seeing a fucking ghost. The thing that blew my mind was that Spike's face looked the same. More than two decades in prison and his face hadn't changed a bit.

I mean, *nobody* thought Spike was ever coming home.

I don't think *Spike* even believed he was coming home.

And the craziest part was how he just touched down without warning. I mean, Spike didn't let anyone know—not even his family.

It was years since his parole hearing, so we figured he was still stuck. We figured he got a denial. The board must have slapped him with a five-year or seven-year denial.

But then suddenly he's out, free as a bird, standing with Al P. on a street in downtown L.A.

I was busy shooting *Law & Order* and didn't get back to L.A. for a minute. I had a concert in Hollywood a few months later and Spike came backstage, but I was moving and grooving, about to perform, and it wasn't until the next morning that we had a chance to chop it up. Me and Coco were staying at the London hotel, Spike came by, and I took him out for breakfast.

Immediately, I was trying to see where his head was at. I have this one question whenever I see cats who've just come out of prison.

Are you *done*?

By that I mean: Are you done testing the system? Are you done challenging the rules? Are you done breaking the motherfucking law?

Because crime is like drugs. It's an addiction. I can't rehab you. Your family can't rehab you. Nobody else can. You have to decide to do it. That's a self-imposed mental place you've got to be at.

We ordered some breakfast. We talked for a few minutes about how he was readjusting to life on the streets. Then I looked him in the eyes.

"Dig, man, are you *done*?"

"Listen," he said. "I'm *done*. No way I'm ever going back."

When he said that, I was studying his facial expression because I can read Spike like a book. I respect him for who he is regardless of the mistakes he's made.

"Ice," he said, "I can't be doing none of that selfish shit no more."

Selfish.

That was a key word for me. That's what I needed to hear.

Because at the end of the day, criminality is the ultimate selfish zone. You want everything and you don't want to work for it. You feel entitled to just go out and take shit. Plus, you think you're smarter than everyone else—that's a toxic mix.

Iceberg Slim said it best: we become "street poisoned."

I sat there with Spike at breakfast, thinking about how we had been on this parallel course. We had been crime partners, out there hitting licks together, but then the music bug bit me, I got out of the game, and our paths diverged.

"I got a pass, Spike. *Somehow*, I got a pass. Hundreds and hundreds of felonies, I ain't never go to prison. All those years in the game, living on that knife's edge. I was always one slip, one mistake, one bad getaway from the penitentiary.

"I'm so lucky in my life today. I got a beautiful wife, a beautiful little daughter. I won't jeopardize that for anything. Dig, man, I won't even jaywalk in New York. I won't spit on the sidewalk. Spike, I feel like if I broke the law today—the way my life has changed—I'd be issued instant karma. I honestly believe that if broke the law, I'd be struck down dead on the spot. I'd have a fucking heart attack or something, you know?"

"Man, I hear you."

I wanted to help Spike out, but from my point of view, there were a bunch of obstacles. I'm very methodical in the way I do shit. One obstacle leads to the next obstacle. I'm like, "Okay, Spike, I'm happy you're out. Where's your head at? You're done testing the system? Cool. You're squared up? If you're done, and you're sincere about living the rest of your life legit, that's one hurdle cleared."

The biggest obstacle I could foresee with Spike was ego. I mean, all players, hustlers, and street cats have this inflated sense of their own importance. They're always saying, "Nigga, I would *never* do that shit." Some basic part of everyday life, some motherfucking thing or another, is always beneath them.

If you're going to function in the real world, you've got to get over that. You've got to be able to swallow your pride.

In the legit world, you have to do what you have to do *before* you can do what you want to do. Street dudes equate that with kissing ass, but in reality it just means you're paying dues, working your way up in the world. When you're in the street, you're a boss and you're out there calling your own shots. But when you get a square job, you're going to have to work your way up the ladder. Spike had been a boss his whole life. In the streets putting together licks, he was in charge.

At first I had my doubts. Could Spike work under people? Could he work his way up? I have a lot of friends who've been bosses their whole lives, but they can't work with me. A lot of street cats come home and can't readjust. I'm cool with them—we're still friends. I just realize they can't function in the legit business world.

Spike made it clear from the jump: "Ice, listen, I ain't no boss. I'm down to do whatever you need me to do, and I'll work my ass off."

I had my eye on Spike for a minute, gauging his attitude, his behavior, even after I was back at work in New York. I'd check in with Al P. and Sean E. Sean and they'd tell me, "Spike's good. His head is in a good place."

Okay, so now the final obstacle is just logistics.

Where can we fit you back in?

We'd resurrected Body Count by the time Spike came home. Ernie C. and I were the only original members left, and we put together a new lineup: Vincent Price on bass, Ill Will on drums, Juan of the Dead on rhythm guitar. I got my son Little Ice doing background vocals and Sean E. Sean working the sampler. In 2014 we dropped our first album in twelve years, *Manslaughter,* and we were busy working on our 2017 album, *Bloodlust.*

I talked to Spike about hitting the road with us. "Well, you can't play no guitar, nigga," I said, "but you can still come on tour. We'll give you a position. We'll make you head of security."

Look, my whole career I never had no bodyguards. I never had a couple of three-hundred-pound paid security dudes, looking like NFL linemen, moving people out of the way and drawing all kinds of stupid-ass attention to me. When it comes to security, I'd rather have a cat who genuinely gives a fuck about me. I'd always prefer to have my friends watching my back.

In 2018, we were planning a European tour with a bunch of dates and festivals, and I had Jorge make sure Spike got his passport, his paperwork straight, and permission from his parole officer to travel.

SPIKE

From the moment we reconnected at that breakfast in Beverly Hills, Ice felt even more like that big-brother figure I needed in my life. Especially now that my two older brothers were dead.

That was a real heart-to-heart. Ice told me that he felt so blessed in life that if he even spit on the curb he'd die on the spot. If he broke the law in any way, God would strike him down. That really hit home with me. I'd certainly felt the sting of karma in my own life.

I told Ice about my grandmother's letter from her deathbed, asking the Heavenly Father to watch over me. I told him that he'd come into my life for a reason—from that first day we met in front of Nat the Cat's house, there was a higher purpose at work. From my point of view at least, our friendship was the Lord's work.

During that whole talk, Ice was letting me know he couldn't be around any kind of negativity—everyone in his inner circle had to be 100 percent legit. I knew he was checking to see if I'd made the inner change. I noticed a lot of changes in him right away, too. He was telling me about his love for his wife and daughter. I absorbed all that and soaked it up like a sponge.

"Damn," I said, "this is a family man."

After we ate, I went up to the hotel room and met Coco. I could see they've got a beautiful relationship—they're in love, of course, but Coco also manages Ice's day-to-day schedule. She's his business partner. Sean E. Sean and Al P. were there in the hotel room, and we all talked for about an hour.

That was probably the biggest difference I noticed, how tight the circle around Ice had gotten. Back in the days of the Rhyme Syndicate and the Old Crime Crew, we'd roll around with thirty or forty motherfuckers. By 2017, the crew was down to three or four dudes: Sean E. Sean, Al P., and when Ice's on the East Coast, Mickey Bentson—just the core guys who've been down with Ice forever.

When I was doing my life sentence, I used to dream of traveling the world. I'd been all over the U.S. and to Hawaii before I fell, but I'd never traveled internationally. In fact, in 1993, Body Count was about to do its first tour of Europe and I was supposed go with them—but then I was arrested and convicted in San Diego. I vividly remember sitting there in my cell in Calipatria thinking that was another thing I'd fucked up—I blown my opportunity to see the world.

But I got a second chance. Ice made it happen for me in the summer of 2018. He gave me a position, put me in charge of security for the band. I hadn't been waiting around for anyone's help—I'd already found myself a job working for a national hardware chain. Pretty quickly I worked my way from part-time to full-time and eventually to supervising a department. But when the opportunity to tour with Body Count came up, I jumped at it. I got my first passport ever. I cleared everything with my parole officer. We went over to Denmark, Holland, Germany, Czech Republic, Poland, Luxembourg, Serbia, Croatia, Sweden, and Switzerland.

When Body Count tours, the energy level is off the charts. Every show, I'm right on stage with the band. I'm not doing one-armed push-ups like in the old Rhyme Syndicate days, but I've got various assigned tasks throughout the show.

"Head of security" is just a title because I'm the *whole* security team for the band. My job is basically to coordinate with the heads of security at the different venues. I'll tell them how we want things organized, how Ice and the band should get from the tour bus through the crowd, and how to make sure everything runs smoothly. At these huge festivals like Hellfest in France or Wacken Open Air in Germany, you look out at a sea of people, close to a hundred thousand fans, and the mosh pit is just insane. With that number of people in one place, you don't want to leave any details to chance. The entrance and exit logistics are crucial. I'm also there to look out for Coco and Chanel—or if Little Ice wants to go someplace after-hours, I'll go with him and make sure nobody starts no bullshit.

For me, the most unforgettable thing of that summer tour was the sightseeing we did on the days between shows. I made it a point to use our downtime to see stuff I'd only read about in books or seen in documentaries. We did concerts in Krakow and Warsaw, and I heard a few of the guys were planning to go see Auschwitz. I said, "I'm definitely going." Just setting foot inside Auschwitz leaves you speechless. You see the railway tracks where the Nazis brought the cattle cars, the showers, the ovens—it really leaves you without words. I'd read about it in history class, but it's different when you see it and experience it in person.

For me, the whole tour was a big history lesson.

Two years earlier, I had been behind the fence in Corcoran. Now I was taking photos on the Charles Bridge in Prague—one of the most beautiful cities I've ever seen. I was in Luxembourg, sitting in one of the oldest castles in Europe. Me and Trome were on bicycles in Sweden—neither of us able to read the road signs—looking up at the snow caps, saying, "It's like in the movies, but the movies don't really do it justice."

Sometimes, when we're out experiencing these things on tour, I feel like I'm living a dream. It reminds me of God's scriptural promise in the book of Malachi, 3:10:

> *I will open the windows of heaven for you. I will pour out a blessing so great you won't have enough room to take it in.*

All the layers of life I've experienced since I came out—man, it feels like a *different* life.

It feels like I truly *was* reborn.

ICE

That's one of the beautiful things about music—it has taken me around the world. Music's opened my eyes to places and people and ideas I never could have imagined.

The stage I'm at now in my life, besides looking after my wife and kids, helping my friends is the most important thing I can do. From the time of my very first tour in 1987, I always wanted to get my dudes away from whatever place they were stuck at. Being in the hood in L.A. all the time is depressing. Dudes grow up in South Central and practically never leave the neighborhood. Look, if Spike got a bunch of money tomorrow, ain't no motherfucking way he's going to use it travel to Sweden or Luxembourg or the Czech Republic. None of my friends would have seen *any* of these places except by coming on tour.

With music, you get to see the globe and it changes your whole perspective on life. These dudes I grew up with—these dudes who are family to me—they tour with Body Count and that's an education in itself. Without even realizing it, traveling broadens your understanding of the planet. Honestly, I think that's the biggest gift I can give them.

"Uncle Spike." That's what my kids call him. And for me, basically, that's Spike's role when Body Count tours—I mean, he's always got some logistical shit to handle, but he's really there to be a protective uncle. That's all I really want him doing, making sure Coco and Chanel are safe and looked after. Most of the time he's moving them around—getting them situated, escorting them in and out of the venue. During our 2018 tour, when Chanel was just two, I would bring her onstage, before we performed "Talk Shit, Get Shot," and I would trust Spike with watching her. I've got enough on my mind, being the front man in a band onstage at these shows with seventy-five thousand or a hundred thousand pumped-up metalheads. It puts my mind at ease knowing that Spike's not going to let anything happen to my wife and kids.

During the show, Spike does whatever needs to be done. He makes sure the guys in the band have what they need—water, towels, whatever. I mean, he's definitely checked his ego and shown he can do whatever's needed. If Little Ice wants to go hang out someplace after the show, Spike goes along to make sure nothing gets lost in translation.

Loyalty. That's such a rare motherfucking commodity these days. *True* loyalty. Lifelong loyalty. Loyalty is probably the trait I value above any other. You've got to remember, being orphaned and having no brothers and sisters, all I've ever had in life is my friends. My friends have always been my family. So I've always been a loyal cat.

My only rule is this: Have you crossed me?

Over the years a lot of motherfuckers *have* crossed me. Dudes I thought were my friends have done me dirty. I'm not talking about a disagreement or a bad moment—that ain't a cross. A cross is an intentional attempt to fuck you.

Spike has never crossed me. So why wouldn't I be loyal?

My attitude is: "Dude, you made some bad mistakes, you went away for all those years and paid your debt to society. Now you're home. I can see you've changed a lot—and changed for the better. I can see your head is in the right place. Okay, come back on board with the team—let's put in some work."

SPIKE

I only go out with Body Count when there's a tour, and that's just occasionally.

Back home in L.A. I work in a large hospital five days a week. I'm an orderly. It doesn't pay a lot, but what I love about it is, I'm helping people. We get a lot of elderly folks suffering with cancer—I'm pushing them in wheelchairs, bringing them into the operating room on gurneys, comforting them in the last weeks of their lives. I'm doing stuff I never thought I'd do, and it feels good to be helping.

When I told Ice about my job, he said, "It's a kind of restitution, Spike, don't you think?"

"Yeah," I said, "it is a kind of restitution."

I can never undo the damage I did. A young man lost his life in a crime I planned—and there's nothing I can ever do to fully pay that back. He didn't deserve to die that way. His family didn't deserve all the pain they've endured.

I can never fix all the hurt I caused. What I can do is try to give back something.

I can give back by living a decent and compassionate life. Sometimes in the hospital halls, people I don't even recognize stop me and say, "Hey, thank you!"

"Excuse me?"

"You helped my father and my family the other day."

"Oh, yeah. It was my pleasure. God bless you."

I'm thinking, *Wow, people really remember the little things you do*. You can help an eighty-year-old person who's recovering from surgery; you can sit there with him and say a few kind words. Maybe you talk about the Dodgers game when you're wheeling him in the elevator, or just keep him company when he's in pain waiting to go into the E.R.

Kindness costs us nothing and can mean everything to people who are hurting.

Sometimes, it feels like I'm fulfilling my grandmother's dying prayer that I would turn from the life of sin and serve God again. I don't know if you'd call it karma, but since I got home, I've been living a good life—I've been so blessed.

After a couple of years of my touring and working with Body Count, the band won the 2021 Grammy in the category Best Metal Performance for their song "Bum Rush."

I'll never forget the morning of Friday, July 30, 2021. At around ten thirty, Ice's manager, Jorge, texted me that he was showing up at my job—it took me completely by surprise.

I rushed outside just as he pulled up in front of the hospital, not in his usual Benz but in a rental car, and told me to jump in the passenger side. He had a super-serious expression on his face—and at first, I was really concerned.

"Jorge, I can't go anywhere, man—I'm just clocking in to my job."

"This will just take a second," Jorge said impatiently.

He pulled his car around the corner.

"Ice sent me to tell you something, Spike. He said you've got to hold on to this red box for him."

"What, Jorge?"

"Spike, don't look in this damned box or tell anyone you've got it. We clear? Just hold it until you get instructions from Ice."

"Okay, Jorge," I said. "Understood."

"Okay, man. Grab it. I've got to get out of here."

Jorge seemed kind of paranoid and pointed to the box in the back seat.

"Okay, okay," I said.

I turned to the back seat, grabbed the small red box, and then Jorge reached over and suddenly pulled off the top.

Inside, carefully wrapped in tissue paper, was my own personal Grammy award.

"Congratulations, Spike," Jorge said, finally cracking a smile. "You truly deserve this—you're as much a part of the Body Count family as anyone."

That meant the world to me. Although I don't play drums or bass or guitar, it told me that my hard work organizing band security, along with the personal responsibilities Ice-T trusted me with—guarding and protecting his family—didn't go unnoticed.

And in my own family life, I've been blessed beyond measure. I met a beautiful young lady named Jasmine Marquez about a year after I paroled out. We fell in love and in 2018, God blessed us with a son, Alton Amir Pierce. He's almost three now. When I wake up, I sometimes sit back and look at my wife and son with tears in my eyes.

Am I dreaming? Did I really get a second chance?

I only wish my mother had lived long enough to meet my son, but it wasn't in God's plan. Her Alzheimer's had progressed quickly, and she passed away on July 25, 2018, one month before Amir was born. Her passing left me heavy-hearted, disappointed in myself, consumed by guilt. I kept reminding myself that more than twenty-five years of me being absent—locked up in the prison system—was the equivalent of me abandoning her.

To make matters worse, even after paroling and coming home,

I never got to see my mom alive again. My mom was living with my sister in another city, and it wasn't logistically possible for me to visit her. The next time I saw her face, she was lying in a casket in a mortuary, and I was left to deal with the pain of having lost someone so dear to me. In my mind there were so many regrets. One thing is for certain: there were countless ripple effects from my bad choices and decisions.

On the other hand, because of my sincere transformation, in a remarkable twist it turned out God would allow my son Amir to be born on the same day as my mother. My son and my late mother share the same birthday, August 24. Though she's no longer here, I know she's looking down on me from above, proud of the positive changes I've made.

I know that she can see I am her son once again.

I've paid a steep price for my bad decisions. I've paid with my freedom and with the damage I did to my own family, especially the pain I've caused my daughter. When I went to prison, she was seven; when I got out, she was thirty-one. She'd had three kids when I was away. I came home the grandfather of three grandchildren I'd never met.

Was any of it worth it? Hell no. All the pain and hurt I caused my mom and grandmother: you can't bring these people back—you can't bring back the time with them you lost. When I went to prison, everyone in my big family of four boys and three girls was still living, all nine of us.

Now both my parents are dead.

My two older brothers are dead.

Two of my sisters are dead.

It's just me and one sister living in Hemet, California. My youngest brother, Dwayne Pierce, is in prison doing a life sentence. All the time I ask myself, "What if I'd been living right in the first place?" Working a regular job, helping people like I'm doing at the hospital? What if I'd been patient enough to get my music career off the ground? I mean, there's so many what-ifs.

Not a day goes by when I don't feel regret and remorse. All I can do is live my life the way I'm living it now. All I can do is be thankful every morning when I open my eyes. All I can do is be thankful I've got my freedom, my family, and a loyal friend like Ice.

Most of all I can be thankful that God's given me the insight to see the errors I made—and the chance to make smarter decisions every single day for the rest of my life.

ICE

I f it costs you your peace, it's too expensive."

I don't know who coined that expression, but it's genius.

The other day I was telling Coco, "I can sleep good at night because I'm not breaking the law. I don't have drugs in this house. I don't have a bunch of cash. I don't have stolen jewelry. There's no reason for anyone to come up in here and do nothing. But if we were criminals, I would be worried about someone kidnapping you. I would be worried about somebody coming here and tying us all up, you know?"

If somebody breaks into my house right now, what the fuck are they going to do—steal a TV off the wall?

You want our money? It's in the bank.

You want our jewelry? It's all insured.

I'm legit, man. I chose the lane that brings peace of mind.

You don't fully realize it until you get out, but honestly the game is a nightmare. The game is *constant* stress. You're always watching your back. You're never really relaxed, you're never really happy. People who don't want to work regular jobs decide they want to play. I've done both, and I can tell you the game is actually a thousand times more stressful than working a square job.

It's great to see Spike mentally in that same place—it's great to see he's legit. Now that he has a wife and a young kid, there's things more important than pride and ego. Fuck the gold chains. Fuck the Rolex. He's focusing on taking care of his little son.

If you think about it, when we were out there wreaking havoc, hitting licks, stealing jewels, we were just showing off. Showing off to women and to each other. None of us was buying houses, none of us was investing. We were living lick to lick. We were a bunch of young dudes just hard-core flossing for each other.

Now we're grown men in our fifties and sixties. Our perspectives have changed and now it's about being there for our families. Stay out of fucking trouble, stay out of fucking jail, and don't make those same mistakes.

When I was a teenager, I used to hang around these older cats, hustlers down at the pool hall. They'd say, "Don't be like me, youngblood." Even *they* knew they were doing wrong! They warn you, but you're too intrigued with their jewelry, their Cadillacs, and the fly women getting into their cars. The game sucks you in. The sexiness and swagger of the criminal life seduce you. Very few people survive it.

It's like an undertow at the beach. You're cocky enough to think you can swim in that water, but it'll pull you under quick.

Before you realize it, you're drowning.

These days, I go talk to kids in schools a lot. Teenagers—thirteen to eighteen—that's the age group you've got to hit if you really want to make a difference. I'll say, "How many of you in the room have a friend that's breaking the law—let's say, selling dope?"

Almost all of them put their hands up.

"Okay, hands down if they're over twenty-five and still doing it."

I watch a bunch of hands drop.

"Over twenty-five and never been to jail."

More hands drop.

"Over thirty, never been to jail, and if they haven't been to jail, somebody close to them has been shot."

By the time I get to thirty-five, all the hands in the room are down.

"Stop and think about that," I say. "Why would you get into an occupation where there's obviously *no* return?"

Well, here's the most common reason:

You're looking for a shortcut. But that shortcut ends up being a long-ass journey through hell, a long-ass journey through these penitentiaries. That shortcut ends up costing you your freedom, decades of your life, maybe all of it.

If you're lucky enough to get paroled like Spike, you might come home in your late fifties. You spent twenty-six years of your life behind the wall, and you'll never get them back. You can work hard as hell, you can live a good life, but can you ever *really* make up for all the life you lost?

Visiting these high schools, I often tell kids the story of me and Spike. The details of our friendship are unique—some of them are stranger than fiction—but in another sense, it's a universal story. What happened to me and Spike has happened thousands and thousands of times before, and it's still happening today.

It's eerie to me how easily our roles could have been reversed.

I could easily have been the guy stuck in the penitentiary for twenty-six years and Spike could have become the star.

We were similar cats—alike in so many ways—heading in the exact same direction. Our lives were so parallel. The only difference was when I hit that fork in the road and made my choice to get out of the game, Spike made his choice to keep speeding in the fast lane—straight toward that fucking cliff.

That's the point I always stress to these kids:

When you hit your own fork in the road, pay attention.

Stop and think about the ramifications.

Think about the consequences.

One slip, one mistake, one bad choice.

That's all it takes.

Sometimes one decision can make all the difference in the world.

ACKNOWLEDGMENTS

SPIKE

I would like to dedicate this book to my grandmother Gladys Burton; my mother, Betty Jean Pierce; my brothers Robert Pierce and Dwayne Pierce; my daughter, Marquise L. Pierce; my grandchildren, Marquel Watkins, Marjhon Watkins, and Marlee Watkins; my wife, Jasmine Marquez; and my son, Alton Amir Pierce-Marquez.

I'd also like to acknowledge the following: my father, Leon Pierce Sr.; my brother Leon Pierce Jr.; my sisters, Gloria Pierce and Tanya Pierce; and my cousins Richard Oliver, John Ross, and Sylvester "Puddin'" Scott.

Obviously, this book project would not have happened were it not for the loyalty and unwavering support of my friend and brother Ice-T. I'd also like to thank Coco Marrow, Chanel Marrow, Tesha Marrow, and Ice Marrow—all of whom are like family to me.

I'm grateful to the members of Body Count, whom I'm proud to count among my closest friends: Ernie Cunnigan, Vince Dennis, Juan Garcia, Will Dorsey Jr., Sean Butler, Oscar Cabrera, Tyler Barber, and David Freeman. RIP Vic "Beatmaster V" Wilson, Mooseman, and D-Roc.

Among the friends I'd like to thank are: Terry "T-Money Bonaventure" Trailer, Al Patrome "Al P." Collins, Joseph NGO, Anthony (Rafik) Hannah, Sharon Grant, Kevin Grant, Steven Grant, Renee Grant, Mark Jolly, Jamo, Tim Kornegay, Alfonzo Tolbert, Tony Jake, Bernard Whitting, Clifton "Clint" Hunter, Shanda Frazier, Deborah Giles, Sheri Beamon, Darryl "Flip" Lawrence, Thaddeus Campbell, Bernard Patton, Jeffrey Thomas, Sean Gordon, Nate "Nat the Cat" Clark, William "Bebop Bill" Clark, Mickey Abbott, Henry "Hen Gee" Garcia, Eric "Evil E" Garcia, Mario "M-Dot" Taylor, Daryl "Shakey" Kilgore, Winsel "Diamond X" Bryant, Dwayne "Frosty Mac" Franklin, Black Whale, John Boy, and Mickey Bentson. RIP Bruce "Burt" Richardson, White Boy Eric, Johnny Parker, and Randy Parker.

I'd also like to express sincere gratitude to my attorney, Keith Watley—who believed in me and helped me in some of my darkest hours.

Finally, I'd like to give my deep thanks to Jorge Hinojosa, Ice's manager, and to Douglas Century, who collaborated so closely with Ice and me to bring our stories to life and make this book a reality.

DOUGLAS CENTURY

I'd like to acknowledge the entire team at Gallery Books for their hard work and dedication to this project: Jeremie Ruby-Strauss, Molly Gregory, Caroline Pallotta, Allison Green, Jamie Selzer, Jennifer Robinson, Bianca Salvant, John Vairo, Lisa Litwack, Jen Bergstrom, Aimée Bell, Jen Long, and Sally Marvin.

ACKNOWLEDGMENTS

Principally, I'd like to express my thanks to my friend Ice for inviting me to be part of this project—and to Spike for sharing so much time and energy in making sure we got his story down correctly. Jorge Hinojosa, who has managed Ice his entire career, was instrumental in making sure every part of this writing and publishing process stayed on course. I'm extremely grateful for the time and energy of my assistant, Natalie Robson, and for the constant loving support of my mother, Marcia Century, and my daughter, Lena Century.

CREDITS

CREDITS

"Bowels Of The Devil"
Words and Music by Ernest T. Cunnigan and Tracy Lauren Marrow
©1992 Rhyme Syndicate Music & Universal Polygram Int. Publishing, Inc.
on behalf of itself and Ernkneesea.
Music Used by Permission—All Rights Reserved

"Don't Hate the Playa" by Tracy Marrow and Richard Ascencio
©1999 Rhyme Syndicate Music and Ringleader Funk Music
Used by Permission—All Rights Reserved

"Make the Loot Loop" by Tracy Marrow and Richard Ascencio
©1996 Rhyme Syndicate Music and Ringleader Funk Music
Used by Permission—All Rights Reserved

"I Must Stand"
Words and Music by Tracy Marrow and Santiago Sanguillen
©1996 Rhyme Syndicate Music and Black Latin Music
Used by Permission—All Rights Reserved

"Forty Days and Forty Nights" Written by Spike
Used by Permission—All Rights Reserved

"Outside Looking In" Written by Spike
Used by Permission—All Rights Reserved